ISLAMOPHOBIA IN HIGHER EDUCATION

ISLAMOPHOBIA IN HIGHER EDUCATION

Combating Discrimination and Creating Understanding

Edited by Shafiqa Ahmadi and Darnell Cole

Foreword by Shaun R. Harper

STERLING, VIRGINIA

Published by Stylus Publishing, LLC.
22883 Quicksilver Drive
Sterling, Virginia 20166-2019

Library of Congress Cataloging-in-Publication Data

Names: Ahmadi, Shafiqa, editor. | Cole, Darnell, editor.

Title: Islamophobia in higher education : combating discrimination and creating understanding / edited by Shafiqa Ahmadi and Darnell Cole ; foreword by Shaun Harper.

Description: First edition. | Sterling, Virginia : Stylus Publishing, 2020. | Includes bibliographical references and index.

Identifiers: LCCN 2020007711 | ISBN 9781620369746 (hardcover) | ISBN 9781620369753 (paperback) | ISBN 9781620369760 (pdf) | ISBN 9781620369777 (ebook)

Subjects: LCSH: Discrimination in higher education--United States. | Islamophobia--United States. | Muslim college students--United States.

Classification: LCC LC212.42 .I73 2020 | DDC 378.1/9828297--dc23

LC record available at https://lccn.loc.gov/2020007711

13-digit ISBN: 978-1-62036-974-6 (cloth)
13-digit ISBN: 978-1-62036-975-3 (paperback)
13-digit ISBN: 978-1-62036-976-0 (library networkable e-edition)
13-digit ISBN: 978-1-62036-977-7 (consumer e-edition)

Printed in the United States of America

All first editions printed on acid-free paper
that meets the American National Standards Institute
Z39-48 Standard.

Bulk Purchases

Quantity discounts are available for use in workshops and for staff development.

Call 1-800-232-0223

First Edition, 2020

This book is dedicated to our three children, who are intelligent and full of life. They appreciate, accept, include, and support everyone, even though they live their own lives in the margins and at the intersections that have been in existence for decades—with an African American Christian dad, a descendant of enslaved people in the United States, and an Afghan American Muslim mom, a refugee to the United States. You—Z, R, and E—sit on shoulders of giants, your ancestors are watching over you, but you must also assume the responsibility to eradicate all forms of discrimination to the best of your abilities.

CONTENTS

Khaseem was my first Muslim friend. Our relationship engendered healthy disturbances in my religious socialization. I was 28 when we met. For 28 years, I had been a serious Christian—at 44, I still am. My father has been a pastor in the African Methodist Episcopal Church for nearly 4 decades; my mother is extremely religious as well. Because of them, I grew up in church. Neither my family nor anyone else ever taught me to hate or in any other way dislike persons from other religious groups. They did teach me, however, that a belief in Jesus Christ was the only way to God, heaven, salvation, and so on. The message, as I interpreted it, was that other religious groups were inferior and somehow wrong, and that ours was right. This socialization, as I understand it now, is a common brand of Christian supremacy. Was it explicitly hateful? Perhaps. Was it implicitly Islamophobic? Definitely so. A delightful, unexpected encounter with a young Muslim man began the process of disrupting these beliefs for me.

I was presenting at a national professional conference; Khaseem was a graduate student attending my session. He approached me at the end. I had no idea he was Muslim, but it was immediately apparent to me that he was kind, thoughtful, smart, and extremely promising. He was also courageous. He asked me, a complete stranger whom he was meeting for the very first time, if I had a summer internship opportunity I could offer him. At the time, he was pursuing a master's degree in upstate New York; I was a professor in Southern California. I gently responded to his internship query with some version of, "Unfortunately, not at this time." I did not deliberately discard him, but the commitment to bring an intern across country within 3 months of our first encounter felt logistically unworkable. Plus, I had no money for an intern, at least not right then. I think Khaseem actually expected me to say no; his reaction to my response was gracious. I invited him to keep in touch; he followed up within weeks. Coincidentally, I was in a meeting with my staff at the time. We had too much work; a colleague suggested we hire an intern. I swiftly made an offer to Khaseem. Miraculously, we somehow figured out the money and logistics. I still did not know he was Muslim. Fifteen years later, I am convincing myself that it would not have made a difference—I sincerely hope I am right and honest about this.

Khaseem had come west to learn from me, but it is likely that I ended up learning more from him. Upon his arrival, I discovered that he was Muslim. To be sure, I know he had not deliberately withheld details about his faith prior to this; it just never came up in our focused conversations about the internship. I recall being intrigued. This was just 3 years after 9/11. Narratives about Muslim people were especially intense and troublesome at that time. Although I had no prior relationships with Muslims, I knew for sure that the ways they were being profiled, policed, harassed, and hated were inconsistent with my Christian values. But even still, all I really knew about them is that they were not Christian. Khaseem inspired me in numerous ways. He was so disciplined about praying. I remember frequently thinking, "Wow, I wish I were as disciplined about praying every day, multiple times each day like him." Khaseem was also a reader. We had such substantive conversations about literature pertaining to Black people. Though I was the one with a PhD, he was the one who brought the deepest analysis to our conversations. I was also inspired by Khaseem's love for his wife, whom he had left behind on the east coast for the summer. I was single at the time. I wanted to love someone (in my case, a man) the way that Khaseem loved his wife. It felt much like the love that pastors preach about in Christian churches, and the love that Christians say one should have for a spouse (sans the homophobia and heterosexism in Christian teachings).

Because I had never had substantive interactions with a Muslim person, I wanted to be especially respectful. I made sure to respect Khaseem's prayer time. I respectfully avoided bringing problematic Christian-centric perspectives to our conversations. When we were in car rides together, I chose to play songs that had no curse words (which remains atypical for me). I remember taking him to dinner once and ordering an appetizer that contained bacon. He took a bite, asked if it had pork, and discreetly spat it out. I was horrified and apologized profusely. I felt so terrible because I knew how important adherence to his faith principles was. Consistent with every other interaction I had with him, Khaseem was kind and forgiving. Honestly, I would have been far more upset were it me. The grace he afforded me in that accidental experience was the kind of grace the Bible tells me Christians are supposed to have. I had fallen short of that grace many, many times—and still do. This one time and in countless others, Khaseem, without trying, modeled for me what I had been taught were the behavioral characteristics of Jesus Christ. The one obvious difference was that he was not Christian. The more time we spent together, the more important that difference became to me. I elaborate on this next.

In writing about the origins of my now 16-year friendship with Khaseem, I am actively resisting three tropes. The first relates to Gordon Allport's well-known contact hypothesis. It is too simplistic to conclude that a lifetime of problematic attitudinal socialization can be easily undone by having contact with a person who is different. Ours was not "contact"—it was meaningful engagement. It was not isolated to a single summer—it continued long after he returned to Buffalo. I am convinced that had he remained my only Muslim friend, the undoing of Islamophobic beliefs to which I had been socialized for 28 years would have been stifled. Attempting to render our religious differences unimportant and insignificant is the second trope I aim to avoid. I do not admire Khaseem despite him being Muslim. Instead, that he is Muslim deepens my respect and appreciation for him. People sometimes say things like, "I don't care what religion you are, we all are human beings." It absolutely matters to me that Khaseem is Muslim because being Muslim matters so deeply to him.

Finally, a claim of being fully cured of my Islamophobic beliefs is the third trope that I am definitely trying to avoid. Three years after the start of what became a beautiful friendship with Khaseem, I moved to Philadelphia. That was good for me. I continued worshipping in predominantly Black Christian churches during the decade I lived there. Nonetheless, it was helpful for my development to be in a city with such a large Muslim population. I had several students, colleagues, and friends there who were Muslim. I had the pleasure of serving on my student Nina's doctoral dissertation committee; I learned lots from her study on the intersections of race, religion, and gender for Black Muslim women in college. I learned even more from our substantive engagement in the research center I founded and directed at the University of Pennsylvania, where Nina worked as a research associate. Additionally, I spent a week engaging with many Muslim people during my visit to Abu Dhabi, which was a transformative experience for me. Despite having cultivated and sustained such rich relationships with Khaseem, Nina, all the Muslim students I have taught, and all the other Muslim people with whom I have interacted in the United States and abroad, it would be dishonest of me to assert that I have arrived at a final point in my anti-Islamophobic journey. I am at least conscious of the ever-presence of Christian dominance and its corresponding messages concerning people from other faiths. Notwithstanding, I know that I must continue to make Muslim friends and learn more about them and also figure out ways I can more forcefully fight against their oppression and marginalization. The Jesus Christ I know and love expects this of me as a Christian, I am sure. To do this with integrity requires continuous personal confrontation with my own unconscious biases and beliefs concerning Muslim persons.

As noted throughout this book, manifestations of Islamophobia are hateful, oppressive, offensive, and at times, violent. But my own journey helped me recognize that Islamophobia is also implicit and unconscious. In my case, I was Islamophobic in having accepted the belief that my religion was superior, it was the right one, and anyone who does not believe in Jesus Christ was destined for hell. I care about Islamophobia because I care about the Muslim people in my life. I also care about the Muslim people whom I do not yet know or may never know. They are people who are too often on the receiving end of inequity and injustice. When I met Khaseem he was a graduate student in higher education. He now works as a higher education administrator. As a person, professor, and higher education administrator myself, I care about what happens to Khaseem, to other Muslim colleagues, and to Muslim college students. I am indebted to him and all my other Muslim friends for helping start the process of undoing my Islamophobic beliefs. I also appreciate the editors and contributors of this important book for advancing much-needed understandings of Islamophobia in higher education and for proposing powerful recommendations to dismantle it. As a Christian, I stand very much in solidarity with the scholars who have written the consequential pages that follow.

I am lucky to have had rich conversations with Khaseem, Nina, and others, which have helped me to learn about Islam and Muslims. However, there are many students, faculty, staff, and administrators who do not have the privilege of having friends and colleagues who can help them understand the experiences of Muslim students in higher education and how Islamophobia impacts their sense of belonging, mattering, educational experiences, and outcomes. As such, *Islamophobia in Higher Education: Combatting Discrimination and Creating Understanding* offers us all rich insights into issues Muslim students face; how to advocate for this marginalized student population through law, policy, and practice; and how to foster anti-Islamophobic campus environments.

Shafiqa Ahmadi and Darnell Cole, my faculty colleagues and longtime friends, have researched the experiences of Muslim students in higher education for more than 17 years. They have authored several peer-reviewed journal articles and other academic publications on this topic. In this volume, these editors bring together contributors who have expertise in the fields of international human rights, civil rights, criminal law, and higher education. The depth of content knowledge evidenced in each chapter deepens readers' understandings of Islamophobia and its harmful impact on Muslim students from various disciplines and perspectives.

Given the misrepresentation of Muslims in general and Muslim students in higher education specifically, this important book aims to provide students, faculty, staff, student affairs professionals, scholars, and student leaders accurate information about Muslims and Muslim college students. It highlights diversity within the community and explores the effects of various laws and policies in higher education. It illustrates how Muslim college students often navigate stigma and stereotypes fueled by Islamophobic rhetoric. For these and numerous other substantive reasons, I highly recommend *Islamophobia in Higher Education: Combatting Discrimination and Creating Understanding.*

Shaun R. Harper
Clifford and Betty Allen Chair in Urban Leadership
Provost Professor of Education and Business
Founder and Executive Director, USC Race and Equity Center
University of Southern California

ACKNOWLEDGMENTS

Completing this book was difficult, yet rewarding. This book, and much of what we have done in our lives, would not have been possible without the support of our children, who gave us the time and mental space to complete the manuscript, even when we had to work at home, taking time away from spending with them. We love you!

We are eternally grateful to our team at the University of Southern California Rossier Center for Education, Identity, and Social Justice—namely, Alex Atashi, Natalia Ayoub, Noha Ayoub, Sedef Berk, Sally Ching, Liane Hypolite, Yasmin Kadir, Bo Lee, Monica Prado-Garcia, Mabel Sanchez, and Noor Traina. We are fortunate to have such an amazing team who kept us organized, assisted with coauthoring some of the chapters, and did so much more that has helped us succeed in completing this book project and codirecting our center. We are honored to work with you!

We are forever indebted to all those who contributed to this edited book. Thank you, Abiya Ahmed, Parwana Anwar, Alex Atashi, Zulaikha Aziz, Cassie Garcia, Liane Hypolite, Bo Lee, Marwa Rifahie, Mabel Sanchez, and Sama Shah.

A very special thanks to John von Knorring and the rest of the Stylus Publishing team for editorial help, keen insight, and ongoing support in bringing this book to life.

INTRODUCTION

Institutionalized Islamophobia on College Campuses

Shafiqa Ahmadi and Darnell Cole

The First Amendment of the United States Constitution protects individuals' "free exercise" of religion from governmental interference. However, laws such as USA PATRIOT Act, Muslim bans, and Student and Exchange Visitor Information System that are enacted and enforced under the guise of national security become a direct violation of the free exercise of religion clause, especially when the target of these laws is Muslims. Given the national legal and political climate that is entrenched in bigotry, xenophobia, and Islamophobia, colleges and universities are in a position to ensure socially just and inclusive environments and ameliorate the negative impact of enforcement of these laws on Muslim college students.

In 2011, beyond their legal jurisdiction, the New York Police Department initiated undercover surveillance operations at Yale, University of Pennsylvania, Rutgers, Princeton, and 12 other college campuses in the Northeast—a salient example of the realities that Muslim college students face. Amid such overt targeting of Muslim college students, more accurate and involved counternarratives of Muslims are needed, as well as a substantive analysis of how Islamophobia has been institutionalized. A normative yet nonmonolithic view of Muslim college students has to consider the sociocultural construction of their religious and spiritual identity, and the institution's role in shaping their postsecondary experiences. Doing so can offer a critical perspective required for understanding Muslim college students and their experiences on college campuses.

On the precipice of the 2016 presidential election, more than 20% of all nationally reported hate crimes were directly related to religious bias, and at least 24% of those religiously related crimes were documented as anti-Islamic (Federal Bureau of Investigation, 2015). During the same year, many highly selective research institutions like the University of Michigan and the University of Maryland were enmeshed in student protests following the

1

campus screenings of *American Sniper* (Rosenberg, 2015; Svrluga, 2015), a controversial film directed by Clint Eastwood that portrayed Chris Kyle, the most lethal sniper in American history, as a broken hero, while simultaneously debasing the complexity of the Iraq War and portraying Muslim non-military combatants as savages. Although student leaders of Muslim Student Unions and Muslim Student Associations spoke out against the religious bias that the movie sparked, the resulting backlash targeted Muslim students as anti-American. Although Muslim student groups like the ones mentioned are established in part to debunk misperceptions, promote inclusion, and build community, the non-Muslim student reaction to their Muslim peers and a legitimate critique of the film typifies how Muslim students are misunderstood on college campuses. The triple murder of Muslim college students in 2015 near the University of North Carolina, Chapel Hill, and the Muslim travel ban's (i.e., Executive Order 13,769 [2017]) impact on students and faculty from the Middle East and North Africa also serve as stark reminders that religious violence and exclusion are all too real (Ahmed & Shoichet, 2015; Amini, 2017). The convergence of religious bias, Islamophobia, and xenophobia in the targeting of Muslims nationally requires a thoughtful investigation as to the extent to which Muslim students experience stigma and discrimination within higher education institutions. It is imperative that such empirical examinations and research scholarship be both relevant to and critical of the laws that inform institutional policy and practice so that college campuses can be cultivated into environments where Muslim students thrive (Ahmadi, Sanchez, & Cole, 2019).

On June 10, 2017, the American Congress for Truth (ACT), an alt-right hate group, organized an anti–shari'a law and, by extension, an anti-Muslim protest in 28 cities across the United States. Armed militia groups accompanied ACT as peacekeepers alongside local police. Although these protests were met with counterprotests, including many college students, the fact that a neo-Nazi, alt-right hate group like ACT could protest against law-abiding Muslim citizens in 2017, with militia acting as peacekeepers, seems to be the new normal in what is being described as Trump-era America (Beydoun, 2018). Though the protests may be constitutionally protected, it is difficult to believe that in 2017 we did not learn from our history of protecting hate at the individual, institutional, and structural levels by law, policy, and political rhetoric. As a consequence, without counternarratives and a focus on the institutionalization of Islamophobia, this new normal becomes part of the discourse for how non–Muslim Americans view Muslims, particularly young Muslim adults attending today's colleges and universities. The common thread of Muslim college students' experiences is navigating stigma and stereotypes laced with Islamophobic rhetoric. To establish as well as foster a socially just campus requires a greater understanding of Muslim college students and how various forms of institutionalized Islamophobia impact Muslims. It is within this sociopolitical and sociocultural context that we offer this book.

Diversity Within the Muslim Population in the United States and College

The Pew Research Center estimates that approximately 3.45 million Muslims were living in the United States during 2017, which meant that 1.1% of the total U.S. population identified as Muslim (Mohamed, 2018). California, Florida, Texas, New York, Illinois, Pennsylvania, Ohio, and North Carolina are states with the most significant percentage of Muslims, per state population estimates (Diamant & Gecewicz, 2017). Nearly half of all Muslims (44%) are between the ages of 18 and 29; 65% are men. Additional findings provided by Pew predict that over the next three decades, the U.S. Muslim community will likely double, and worldwide, Muslims will become the largest religious group, surpassing Christians (Diamant & Gecewicz, 2017).

The Pew Research Center (2017) also estimates that about 54% of Muslims hold a college degree, with 11% of those being postgraduate degrees (Diamant & Gecewicz, 2017). An earlier Pew report indicated, "Religious minorities often have more education, on average, than a country's majority religious group, particularly when the minority group is largely foreign-born and comes from a distant country" ("Large Gaps in Education Levels Persist," 2016). Muslims

> are much more likely than Christians to have post-secondary degrees. And unlike Christians, large majorities of Hindus and Muslims were born outside the United States (87% of Hindus and 64% of Muslims compared with 14% of Christians, according to a 2014 Pew Research Center survey). ("Large Gaps in Education Levels Persist," 2016)

Smith's (2001) research corroborates these findings, as he also notes that Muslims are generally younger and better educated than the general public, and the number of Muslims among college students is proportionately higher than the numbers within the general population. Of the total number of students attending four-year colleges in these reports, 0.9% were estimated to be Muslim (Bagby, Perl, & Froehle, 2001; Smith, 2001). Today's estimates have likely increased. Although the numerical representation of Muslims in college provides a useful frame for this book's topic, it is also necessary to understand the sociopolitical and sociocultural context of Muslim students in American higher education, which requires empirical inquiry and intellectual discourse.

Purpose and Scope of This Book

The impact of college on students, particularly on the educational gains received as a result of their experience, continues to drive institutional policy. The religious identification of college students, especially for Muslims, has had relatively little attention in higher education literature on the nature of student experiences in U.S. colleges and universities, as well as the institutional policies and practices that shape those experiences (Ahmadi et al., 2019; Cole & Ahmadi, 2010). Although recent legal, political, and social values prized by the Christian right have made gains on the value center of mainstream America, it was not until the more recent national and subsequently global attention on terrorist acts of Islamic extremists that students' religious identities became a concern for national security. Such direct links between religious identity and national security have created gross overgeneralizations, misinformation, and subsequent inhospitable environments for many Muslims in the United States.

Unfortunately, many of these inhospitable environments exist on college and university campuses. Concomitantly, colleges and universities have often provided a context for debate, opportunities to voice social and political viewpoints, student protest, and the intellectual scholarship supporting or condemning not only acts of terrorism but also America's response to those acts. It is within this sociopolitical and georeligious context that we examine the laws, policies, and identity of Muslim students in American higher education institutions. Implications for institutional policy and practice are also provided toward reducing monolithic portrayals of Muslims and institutionalized Islamophobia to reform the college context and improve the ways in which laws and policies are turned into professional practice.

The purpose of this book is threefold: (a) to examine how Islamophobia has been institutionalized in postsecondary institutions, (b) to consider the extent to which other social identities have been ignored and yet illuminate a critical intersection between Islamophobia and institutional policy, and (c) to offer recommendations for improving institutional policy and professional practice. Although it is important to debunk stereotypes, correct misperceptions, and inform the misinformed, it is more critical in this era of falsehoods or "fake news" to generate accurate information and discourse that allows for meaningful analyses of institutionalized Islamophobia. Researchers, scholars, and professionals in higher education often ignore or minimize social and political events, as well as religious identity, when examining students' college experiences and the resultant impact on their educational gains, satisfaction, perspectives, and religious identity. As a result, educators have had relatively little research or critical analyses in understanding Islamophobia and the institutional practices that foster it and the resultant impact on Muslim students and the institutional context of college. Given the intentional misrepresentation and miseducation about Muslims in general, and Muslim students in higher education specifically, this book seeks to provide students, faculty, staff, student affairs professionals, scholars, and student leaders with accurate information about Muslims and Muslim college student experiences. Moreover, each chapter in this book addresses how institutions of higher education can better serve Muslim college students through changing law, policy, and practice to disrupt Islamophobia on their college campuses. Each chapter ends with discussion questions for in-class activity.

Organization of This Book

This edited book highlights the diversity within the Muslim community and explores how various laws and policies affect Muslim college students. The contributors in this book represent different voices whose work on this marginalized student population is traditionally not recognized within academic settings, such as an international human rights attorney, a civil rights attorney, and a criminal attorney, as well as more traditional higher education scholars who are student affairs practitioners and research faculty. Moreover, the voices of female Muslim scholars, in particular, are highlighted. Invited contributors work directly in the field and have previously produced valuable discussions in this area with the editors.

The book is organized into eight chapters. The first chapter, titled "Muslim Bans: Impact of Exclusionary Policies on Muslim College Students," is by Marwa Rifahie, a public defender for LA County. She previously served as a civil rights attorney at the Council on American-Islamic Relations, Greater Los Angeles Office. This chapter discusses Islamophobia and its relation to civil rights, specifically the harmful impact of the Muslim bans on Muslim college students. Chapter 2, titled "Criminalization of Muslim Students Post-9/11," is by Parwana Anwar, a trial and criminal defense attorney. Anwar examines the process of criminalization and the double standards of the legal system regarding the ways in which Muslim students are unfairly treated. Chapter 3, "The Muslim Bans, Human Rights, and International Muslim Students," is by Zulaikha Aziz, a human rights attorney and assistant professor of the practice at the School of International Relations at the University of Southern California (USC). This chapter explores the Muslim bans within the legal context of international conventions barring discrimination and the negative implications of the Muslim bans on the experiences of international Muslim college students.

Chapter 4, "Immigrant Status of Muslims," is by Bo Lee, project specialist at the USC Rossier Center for Education, Identity and Social Justice, and Shafiqa Ahmadi, associate professor of clinical education. This chapter briefly discusses the history of immigration laws and policies and specifically explores their impacts on the diverse and intersectional experiences of immigrant-status Muslims on college campuses. Chapter 5, "Queer Muslims," is by Shafiqa Ahmadi and Sama Shah. This chapter explores the diverse and intersectional experiences of queer Muslims and the institutional practices that have shaped and continue to shape their college experiences. Chapter 6, "Black Muslims," is by Darnell Cole, associate professor of education; Liane Hypolite, a USC PhD student; and Alex Atashi, project specialist at USC Rossier Center for Education, Identity and Social Justice. This chapter examines the changing context for laws, policies, and politics that have shaped the Islamophobic tendencies and the subsequent marginality of Black Muslims. Chapter 7, titled "Latinx Muslims," is by Mabel Sanchez, a USC PhD student, and Shafiqa Ahmadi. This chapter provides a brief history of Latinx Muslims in the United States, including their conversion or reversion journeys to Islam and their interactions with their families. Latinx Muslims, described as the "brown threat," are defined and their experiences in the United States are discussed. Chapter 8, the last chapter, is titled "A Home Away From Home: Community Countering Challenges." This chapter, by Abiya Ahmed and Cassie Garcia, provides a case study of how one student affairs–run organization, the Markaz Resource Center at Stanford University, addresses some of the issues raised in the literature and serves as a "home away from home" by creating community for Stanford Muslim-identifying students (as well as including those who do not identify as Muslim).

References

Ahmadi, S., Sanchez, M., & Cole, D. (2019). Protecting Muslim students' speech and expression and resisting Islamophobia. In D. L. Morgan & C. H. Davis, III (Eds.), *Student activism, politics, and campus climate in higher education* (pp. 97–111). New York, NY: Routledge.

Ahmed, S., & Shoichet, C. E. (2015, February 11). 3 students shot to death in an apartment near UNC Chapel Hill. *CNN*. Retrieved from http://www.cnn.com/2015/02/11/us/chapel-hill-shooting/index.html

Amini, M. (2017, February 22). University students left in limbo by Trump's travel ban. *CNBC.* Retrieved from https://www.cnbc.com/2017/02/17/university-students-left-in-limbo-bytrumps-travel-ban.html

Bagby, I., Perl, P. M., & Froehle, B. T. (2001). *The mosque in America: A national portrait, a report from the mosque.* Washington, DC: Council on American-Islamic Relations.

Beydoun, K. A. (2018). *American Islamophobia: Understanding the roots and rise of fear.* Berkeley: University of California Press.

Cole, D., & Ahmadi, S. (2010). Reconsidering campus diversity: An examination of Muslim students' experiences. *The Journal of Higher Education, 81*(2), 121–139.

Diamant, J., & Gecewicz, C. (2017, October). 5 facts about Muslim Millennials in the U.S. *Pew Research Center: Religion and Public Life.* Retrieved from https://www.pewresearch.org/fact-tank/2017/10/26/5-facts-about-muslim-millennials-us/

Exec. Order No. 13,769, 82 Fed. Reg. 8977 (2017).

Federal Bureau of Investigation (FBI). (2017). *Uniform crime report hate crime statistics, 2016: Incidents and offenses.* Retrieved from https://ucr.fbi.gov/hate-crime/2016/topic-pages/incidentsandoffenses.pdf

Large gaps in education levels persist, but all faiths are making gains—particularly among women. (2016, December). *Pew Research Center: Religion and Public Life.* Retrieved from https://www.pewforum.org/2016/12/13/religion-and-education-around-the-world/

Mohamed, B. (2018). *New estimates show U.S. Muslim population continues to grow.* Retrieved https://www.pewresearch.org/fact-tank/2018/01/03/new-estimates-show-u-s-muslim-population-continues-to-grow/

Rosenberg, A. (2015, April 16). The University of Michigan, 'American Sniper,' and the state of college campuses. *Washington Post.* Retrieved from https://www.washingtonpost.com/news/act-four/wp/2015/04/16/the-university-of-michigan-american-sniper-and-the-state-of-college-campuses/?utm_term=.c5c3b41694dd

Smith, T. (2001). *Estimating the Muslim population in the United States.* Retrieved from http://www.ajc.org/InTheMedia

Svrluga, S. (2015, April 28). After backlash, U-Md. groups to screen "American Sniper" and talk it out. *Washington Post.* Retrieved from https://www.washingtonpost.com/news/grade-point/wp/2015/04/28/after-backlash-u-md-groups-to-screen-american-sniper-and-talk-it-out/

MUSLIM BANS

Impact of Exclusionary Policies on Muslim College Students

Marwa Rifahie

Shocking the world, on November 8, 2016, Donald J. Trump became the forty-fifth president of the United States. The reality TV billionaire pulled off what is frequently called the biggest upset in U.S. elections history by winning the presidency after securing the necessary number of electoral votes, despite losing the popular vote. With a presidential campaign that was marked with unabashed bigotry, xenophobia, and incompetence, much of the United States and the international community remained in a state of fear, anxiety, and great uncertainty about what was to come. As the 2016 presidential campaign became rife with Islamophobic rhetoric, many students and university administrators feared the negative impact this mainstream Islamophobia would have on Muslim college students.

Shortly after election night, Kris Kobach, the presidential transition adviser, signaled to a major news network that the president-elect was working to implement different Muslim exclusionary measures (Flores, 2016). In a television interview, Carl Higbie, the former spokesperson for the Trump Great America PAC, used World War II internment of Japanese Americans as precedent for the purported sweeping, targeted treatment of Muslims that was to come from the soon-to-be Trump administration. "It is legal," Higbie argued. "[A Muslim registry] will hold Constitutional muster. . . . We've done it based on race, we've done it based on religion. . . . We did it during World War II with Japanese" (Bromwich, 2016, para. 4). Then, in a separate television interview, Trump reiterated his call for a ban on Muslim immigration, asserting that it had gotten "tremendous support" and that "we're

9

having problems with the Muslims, and we're having problems with Muslims coming into the country" (Hauslohner & Johnson, 2017, para. 22).

If nothing else, the Muslim American community could anticipate that the Trump presidency would be marked with policies and programs built on the premise that Muslim identity is presumptively threatening. The proposed Muslim exclusionary policies have a broader impact on more than just national security and immigration.

> By endorsing the Islamophobic premise that Muslim identity is presumptive of radical threat or terrorism, Islamophobic policies and programs enacted by the state propagate the damaging stereotypes associated with this premise, and promote the private vigilantism that threatens Muslims and communities mistakenly caricatured as Muslims. (Beydoun, 2017a, para. 11)

Private vigilantism and hate crimes against Muslims occurred at an unprecedented rate in 2017, which was set to be one of the worst years ever for such incidents.

The Council on American-Islamic Relations (CAIR), the nation's largest Muslim civil rights and advocacy organization, reported that the number of hate crimes against Muslims in the first half of 2017 spiked 91% compared to the same period in 2016, which was already the worst year for anti-Muslim incidents since CAIR began documenting and reporting them in 2013 (CAIR, 2017). This same uptick is represented in discriminatory incidents against Muslims. A 2017 Pew Research Center study found that 75% of Muslims believed there was "a lot of discrimination against Muslims in the United States" (Pew Research Center, 2017, para. 1).

The purpose of this chapter is to understand the extent to which Islamophobia, the closed-minded prejudice against or hatred of Islam and Muslims, through President Trump's exclusionary Muslim bans has manifested and institutionalized itself into intolerance and discrimination at higher education institutions for Muslim college students. This chapter will also look at how the Muslim ban litigation treated the arguments against exclusion for the sake of academic welfare. Additionally, it will provide policy recommendations and conclude with discussion questions.

Predating Trump: A History of Institutional Criminalization Against Muslim Immigrants

Criminalization, tracking, and heightened screening and vetting are not new ideas that resulted from the current Muslim ban. Rather, they have been objectives of national security policy since 9/11. The Department of Homeland Security and other federal law enforcement agencies have historically implemented programs that are premised on the idea that Muslims are inherently dangerous and suspicious. Muslims have been the targets of entry and exit registration programs, extreme vetting, visa restrictions and cancellations, the No Fly list and other watch lists, and immigration processing delays (Chehata, 2018).

National Security Entry-Exit Registration System

In 2002, approximately one year after the 9/11 terrorist attacks, the Department of Justice (DOJ) announced the National Security Entry-Exit Registration System (NSEERS) program, which required nonimmigrant visa holders such as tourists and students to specially register with immigration officials (Registration of Certain Nonimmigrant Aliens From Designated Countries, 2002). NSEERS mandated the registration of all males over the age of 16 years from any of 25 designated countries who met NSEERS standards; all but one of the designated countries (North Korea) were Muslim-majority. As a result, 80,000 males affected by NSEERS were fingerprinted, photographed, and interrogated about personal details including financial information and family ties (Chehata, 2018). Targeted Muslim immigrants were required to check in regularly with the agency then called Immigration and Naturalization Service (INS). In 2011, the government delisted all 25 countries after determining that it is not "necessary to subject nationals from these countries to special registration procedures" (Removing Designated Countries From the National Security Entry-Exit Registration System, 2011, p. 23,830) and that NSEERS "does not provide any increase in security" (p. 23,831). More than five years later, in December 2016, President Barack Obama dismantled NSEERS in response to suggestions by then President-elect Trump to revive the dormant program in efforts to create a so-called "Muslim Registry" (Patel & Price, 2016).

Student Exchange Information System

After it was reported that one of the individuals from the attacks on 9/11 entered the United States on a student visa, Diane Feinstein, California's Democratic senator, proposed a six-month moratorium on all international student visas (Schemo, 2001). Although the moratorium never went into effect, the sentiment it created helped establish the Student and Exchange Visitor Information System (SEVIS) in 2003. Under SEVIS, universities are mandated to electronically report on international students, effectively turning student advisers into government watchdogs. Criticisms include opinions that "SEVIS will create an atmosphere of intimidation on campus that is intended to silence international students" and that "international students will be barred from student movements, because of fear that alleged student misconduct would be reported in SEVIS and possibly serve as a basis for deportation" (Jackson, 2004, pp. 386–387).

Before the Trump presidency, individuals from Muslim-majority countries experienced increased scrutiny when applying for visas to enter the United States (Chehata, 2018). According to the Brennan Center for Justice at the New York University School of Law, an average of 48.8% of visas were refused from Iran, Libya, Yemen, Somalia, Sudan, and Syria in 2016 (Levinson-Waldman & Patel, 2017). Additionally, based on data released by the U.S. Department of State in April 2017, "the United States issued about 40 percent fewer temporary visas in March [2017] to citizens of seven countries covered by President Donald Trump's temporary travel bans than it did in an average month last year" (Torbati, 2017, para. 1).

In 2015, Congress passed the Visa Waiver Program Improvement and Terrorist Travel Prevention Act, which increased barriers to entry for individuals from designated Muslim-majority countries who were previously eligible for the Visa Waiver Program (VWP) (Chehata, 2018). Dual nationals of Iran, Iraq, Syria, and Sudan, as well as VWP-eligible nationals who in recent years merely traveled to, or were present in, Iraq, Syria, Iran, Sudan, Libya, Somalia, or Yemen, were barred from entering the United States under VWP (Chehata, 2018). "Extreme vetting" policies implemented under the Trump administration in day-to-day practices by immigration officials include reports of invasive questioning of travelers about their religious beliefs, such as whether they are Sunni or Shiite and why they carry a Qur'an in their luggage (Levinson-Waldman & Patel, 2017). This intrusive questioning appears to disproportionately target Muslims and violates immigration laws that protect immigrants' constitutional rights and religious freedom (Chehata, 2018). Government officials under President Trump have indicated that upcoming procedures for visa applicants would include questions regarding "honor killings, the role of women in society, and legitimate military targets" (Levinson-Waldman & Patel, 2017, para. 5), as well as guidelines that require applicants to reveal information in their electronics, such as contacts, social media usernames, and passwords.

The Trump administration has used these policies and restrictions as part of its justification for the institutional framework that creates a discriminatory atmosphere for Muslims, based on unwarranted profiling criteria premised on Islamophobic ideas.

Muslim Ban 1.0

President Donald J. Trump executed his promise to ensure there should be "a total and complete shutdown of Muslims entering the United States" by signing an executive order—Muslim Ban 1.0—entitled "Protecting the Nation From Foreign Terrorist Entry Into the United States" (Executive Order No. 13,769, 2017; see also Hauslohner & Johnson, 2017). Muslim Ban 1.0's stated purpose was to "protect the American people from terrorist attacks by foreign nationals admitted to the United States" (Executive Order No. 13,769, 2017, p. 13). The new measure made several changes to the policies and procedures by which noncitizens may enter the United States. First, Muslim Ban 1.0 suspended for 90 days the entry of aliens from seven countries: Iran, Iraq, Libya, Somalia, Sudan, Syria, and Yemen. Second, Muslim Ban 1.0 suspended the United States Refugee Admissions Program for 120 days. Upon resumption of the refugee program, Muslim 1.0 directed the secretary of state to prioritize refugee claims based on religious persecution where a refugee's religion is the minority religion in the country of his or her nationality. This measure was largely understood to allow Christian refugees, while continuing to block Muslims. Third, Muslim Ban 1.0 suspended indefinitely the entry of all Syrian refugees.

Muslim Ban 1.0 was poorly drafted and improperly implemented, and the chaos it caused was unprecedented. In the first day, without proper guidance from the president, Customs and Border Patrol agents applied the ban to legal permanent residents and dual citizens. Travelers arriving on visas were detained and denied entry into the United States due to the immediate cancellation of their visas. Others were denied boarding on their international flights entering the United States, because airlines were now bearing the expense of mandatory return flights for those denied entry. Muslim Ban 1.0 lasted three days until the state of Washington filed a complaint seeking declaratory and injunctive relief and a motion for a temporary restraining order (TRO) against the president's executive order. The state of Washington's claims for injury relied in great part on the damaging effects Muslim Ban 1.0 had on the state's higher education institutions, particularly the University of Washington and Washington State University, the two largest public research universities in the state. The complaint stated, "More than 95 students from Iran, Iraq, Syria, Somalia, Sudan, Libya, and Yemen attend the University of Washington, based in Seattle. More than 135 students from those countries attend Washington State University" (*Washington v. Trump*, 9th Cir. 2017, para. 17). Moreover, the motion for the TRO argued that Muslim Ban 1.0 disrupts students' personal and professional lives, prevents travel for research and scholarship, and harms the universities' missions. Most notably, the motion for the TRO argued that the Muslim ban undermines "Washington's sovereign interest in remaining a welcoming place for immigrants and refugees" (para. 1).

That same day, the United States District Court for the Western District of Washington issued a nationwide TRO blocking Muslim Ban 1.0's sections on immigrant and nonimmigrant entry (*Washington v. Trump*, W. D. Wash. 2017). The TRO also enjoined the Muslim Ban 1.0 section regarding priority for refugee claims of religious minorities, to the extent that it "purports to prioritize refugee claims of certain religious minorities"; the decision instead prohibited the government from "proceeding with any action that prioritizes the refugee claims of certain religious minorities" (*Washington v. Trump*, 9th Cir., 2017, para. 7). The next day, the Trump administration sought an emergency stay and appealed the district court's decision with the Ninth Circuit Court of Appeals. In its order denying the request for the emergency stay, the Ninth Circuit focused on Washington's argument that Muslim Ban 1.0 caused a concrete and particularized injury to public universities. The court considered the declarations filed by the state of Washington detailing that the teaching and research missions of their universities were harmed by Muslim Ban 1.0's effect on their faculty and students who are nationals of the seven affected countries. The court highlighted the state's argument that "these students and faculty cannot travel for research, academic collaboration, or for personal reasons, and their families abroad cannot visit. Some have been stranded outside the country, unable to return to the universities at all" (*Washington v. Trump*, 9th Cir., 2017, para. 16). For instance, Muslim Ban 1.0 had resulted in a Sudanese Stanford University student being detained at JFK International Airport in New York and an Iranian PhD candidate at Yale University being stranded in Dubai (Kanowitz, 2017).

In response to many of the court losses suffered by the new administration, President Trump vehemently asserted at a February 16, 2017, news conference that Muslim Ban 1.0 was lawful but that a new order would be issued (Almasy & Simon, 2017). Subsequently, Stephen Miller, senior policy adviser to the president, described the modifications to the new Muslim ban order as "mostly minor technical differences," stressing that the "basic policies are still going to be in effect" (Zapotosky, 2017, para. 1). Additionally, White House Press Secretary Sean Spicer stated, "The principles of the [second] executive order remain the same" (Stuart, 2017, para. 1). After humiliating rounds in court blasting Muslim Ban 1.0 as unconstitutional and discriminatory, and in an effort to avoid further litigation, the president enacted a second order—Muslim Ban 2.0—on March 6, 2017, bearing the same name as the previous order (Executive Order No. 13,780, 2017). The supposedly more refined Muslim Ban 2.0 revoked and replaced Muslim Ban 1.0.

Muslim Ban 2.0

Muslim Ban 2.0 sought to reinstate a 90-day suspension of entry for nationals from six countries, eliminating Iraq from the list, but retaining

Iran, Libya, Somalia, Sudan, Syria, and Yemen as the designated countries (Executive Order No. 13,780, 2017). Muslim Ban 2.0 attempted to narrow the suspension of entry by applying it to foreign nationals who (a) were outside the United States on its effective date of March 16, 2017; (b) did not have a valid visa on that date; and (c) did not have a valid visa on the effective date of the first executive order—January 27, 2017 (Executive Order No. 13,780, 2017). Muslim Ban 2.0 explicitly clarified that it did not bar entry of lawful permanent residents, dual citizens traveling under a passport issued by a nondesignated country, asylees, or refugees already admitted to the United States (Executive Order No. 13,780, 2017). Muslim Ban 2.0 also lifted the indefinite ban on Syrian refugees. Although Muslim Ban 2.0 was not a "total and complete shutdown of Muslims entering the United States" (Hauslohner & Johnson, 2017, para. 15) as the president initially pursued, it resulted in continued legal challenges to its constitutionality by individuals, organizations, and states across the country. District court judges in Hawaii and Maryland issued orders temporarily blocking critical sections of Muslim Ban 2.0 before its implementation.

The state of Hawaii, like Washington in its legal proceedings against the Muslim ban, asserted that one of the two proprietary injuries the state would suffer resulted from Muslim Ban 2.0's impact on the University of Hawaii system. Hawaii argued, and the Fourth Circuit agreed, that students and faculty suspended from entry would be barred from studying or teaching at the university, now and in the future, irrevocably damaging their personal and professional lives and harming the educational institutions themselves (*State of Hawaii v. Trump*, 2017). In addition to the expected great financial loss to the University of Hawaii system, Hawaii argued that "the University will suffer serious non-monetary losses, including damage to the collaborative exchange of ideas among people of different religions and national backgrounds on which the State's educational institutions depend" (*State of Hawaii v. Trump*, 2017). The state also noted that universities have a global mission of engagement to rely on visiting students, scholars, and faculty to advance their educational goals. As such, Hawaii further argued, Muslim Ban 2.0 "will impair the University's ability to recruit and accept the most qualified students and faculty, [and] undermine its commitment to being 'one of the most diverse institutions of higher education' in the world" (*State of Hawaii v. Trump*, 2017).

In the Maryland lawsuit, one of the organizational plaintiffs, the Middle East Studies Association (MESA), an organization of students and scholars of Middle Eastern studies, also asserted irreparable harm from Muslim Ban 2.0. MESA's mission statement says that the organization fosters the study of the Middle East, promotes high standards of scholarship and teaching, and encourages public understanding of the region and its peoples through programs, publications and services that enhance education, further intellectual exchange, recognize professional distinction, and defend academic freedom in accordance with its status as a 501(c)(3) scientific, educational, literary, and charitable organization. (MESA, 2017, para. 1)

The ban would make this impossible. MESA also argued that its membership contained nationals from the designated countries, and Muslim Ban 2.0 would make travel impossible for some of its members for academic conferences and fieldwork, and that the inability of its members to enter the United States would cripple its annual conference, on which it relies in large part for its yearly revenue.

The administration appealed the orders to the U.S. Court of Appeals for the Fourth and Ninth Circuits. The district court injunctions were upheld in both appeals courts, which refused to allow Muslim Ban 2.0 to proceed. In a blow to the Trump administration, the Fourth Circuit Court of Appeals stated that the U.S. Constitution should be used to protect the plaintiff's right to challenge "an Executive Order that in text speaks with vague words of national security, but in context drips with religious intolerance, animus, and discrimination" (*IRAP v. Trump*, 4th cir., 2017, p. 2). Moreover, the court noted "the Establishment Clause of the First Amendment yet stands as an untiring sentinel for the protection of one of our most cherished founding principles—that government shall not establish any religious orthodoxy, or favor or disfavor one religion over another" (*IRAP v. Trump*, 4th cir., 2017, p. 2). In clear acknowledgment that the supposedly more refined and constitutional Muslim Ban 2.0 was just as objectionable and unaccepted in the courts as its predecessor, the president sought a writ of certiorari in both the Hawaii and Maryland cases with the U.S. Supreme Court, which was granted.

The U.S. Supreme Court opinion was not shocking when viewed in consideration of post-9/11 Supreme Court jurisprudence related to national security or the War on Terror. Despite the obvious discriminatory intent behind Muslim Ban 2.0 and its glaring unconstitutionality, the Supreme Court decided to practice almost absolute deference to the presidency and lifted the lower court's injunctions except as to foreign nationals who have "credible claim of a bona fide relationship with a person or entity in the United States" (*Trump v. IRAP*, 2017, p. 12). Contributing to more chaos, the Supreme Court did not properly define what would qualify as a *bona fide relationship*. The Supreme Court did state that the plaintiffs in the Maryland and Hawaii cases illustrate the sort of relationship that qualifies. The court attempted to detail persons with a bona fide relationship as follows:

> For individuals, a close familial relationship is required. A foreign national who wishes to enter the United States to live with or visit a family member, like Doe's wife or Dr. Elshikh's mother-in-law, clearly has such a relationship. As for entities, the relationship must be formal, documented, and formed in the ordinary course, rather than for the purpose of evading EO-2. The students from the designated countries who have been admitted to the University of Hawaii have such a relationship with an American entity. So too would a worker who accepted an offer of employment from an American company or a lecturer invited to address an American audience. Not so someone who enters into a relationship simply to avoid §2(c): For example, a nonprofit group devoted to immigration issues may not contact foreign nationals from the designated countries, add them to client lists, and then secure their entry by claiming injury from their exclusion. (*Trump v. IRAP*, 2017, p. 12)

Although the Supreme Court made it clear that spouses and parents-in-law could establish a bona fide relationship to a person in the United States, the Trump administration took it perhaps too literally. The Trump administration interpreted the Supreme Court's decision as limiting entry to only parents, children, spouses, parents-in-law, sons- and daughters-in-law, people engaged to be married, and siblings (Liptak, 2017). Missing from the Trump administration's interpretation were grandparents, grandchildren, aunts, uncles, nieces, nephews, cousins, brothers-in-law, and sisters-in-law.

This narrow interpretation was also subject to legal challenges in district court in Hawaii, again, as the state of Hawaii argued that the government was seeking to implement a narrower construction of a bona fide relationship than that intended by the Supreme Court. The District Court of Hawaii held:

> In sum, the Government's definition of "close familial relationship" is not only not compelled by the Supreme Court's June 26 decision, but contradicts it. Equally problematic, the Government's definition represents the antithesis of common sense. Common sense, for instance, dictates that close family members be defined to include grandparents. Indeed, grandparents are the epitome of close family members. The Government's definition excludes them. That simply cannot be. (*State of Hawaii v. Trump*, 2017, pp. 14–15)

The Supreme Court upheld the Hawaii district court's expansion of the definition of a *bona fide relationship*.

Facing the impending decision on Muslim Ban 2.0, the Trump administration should have, at this point, realized that district courts, appeals courts, and even the Supreme Court would block any attempt to bar entry of foreign nationals seeking to, and who have been admitted to, attend universities in the United States. Even in the Supreme Court's bizarre "bona fide relationship" order, the court specifically acknowledged "the students from the designated countries who have been admitted to the University of Hawaii have such a relationship with an American entity" (*Trump v. IRAP*, 2017, p. 12).

Muslim Ban 3.0

On September 24, 2017, the day on which Muslim Ban 2.0's prohibition on foreign nationals from Iran, Libya, Somalia, Sudan, Syria, and Yemen was set to expire, President Trump issued a proclamation—Muslim Ban 3.0—that imposed new travel restrictions on the entry of foreign nationals from Chad, Iran, Libya, North Korea, Somalia, Syria, Venezuela, and Yemen. Muslim Ban 3.0 had a commencement date of October 18, 2017. Perhaps emboldened by the Supreme Court's ruling on Muslim Ban 2.0, the president's new proclamation resulted in indefinite restrictions on travel for foreign nationals from the designated countries. The restrictions were also no longer uniform across all the designated countries, and the ban distinguishes between entry as an immigrant—meaning those who are seeking admission to the United States on a permanent basis through a family member, U.S. employer, or through the Diversity Lottery Program—and a nonimmigrant—meaning those who are seeking admission into the United States on a temporary basis, such as business visitors, tourists, students, exchange students, scholars, and temporary workers. More specifically, Muslim Ban 3.0 restricted U.S. entry from each of the designated countries as follows: (a) for North Korea and Syria, a complete ban on issuance of immigrant and nonimmigrant visas; (b) for Iran, a complete ban on immigrant visas and nonimmigrant visas except for nonimmigrant visas for students and exchange visitors after enhanced screening and vetting; (c) for Libya, Yemen, and Chad, a complete ban on immigrant, business, and tourist visas; (d) for Somalia, a complete ban on immigrant visas, and applications for nonimmigrant visas would be subjected to additional scrutiny; and (e) for Venezuela, only a ban on business and tourist visas for certain government officials and their immediate families. Subsequently, on October 10, 2017, the Supreme Court vacated the Fourth Circuit's order concerning the 90-day ban on foreign nationals from the designated countries as moot, because the 90-day period had expired.

Although President Trump's Muslim Ban 3.0 adopts a more tailored approach than the previous iterations and appears to recognize the value of educational exchanges—especially with higher education institutions—it does not fully remedy the detrimental effects the Muslim ban will have on higher education institutions and academia. As stated by Jill Welch, the deputy executive director for public policy at NAFSA: Association of International Educators,

> For example, researchers from Chad, Libya and Yemen may no longer be able to attend a U.S. conference, and other nonimmigrant travelers from the additional countries named will be subjected to yet further enhanced screening and vetting. Such an approach only helps fuel the ongoing uncertainty felt by students, scholars and other travelers from across the world since the first travel ban took effect in January. Again, true security lies in understanding the nature of specific threats and focusing on individuals who mean to cause us harm—not in preventing entire nationalities from entering the United States. (Redden, 2017, para. 8)

The selection of the ban on student, exchange student, and scholar-based nonimmigrant visas for certain designated countries seems arbitrary. Syria and North Korea are subject to a complete ban, including students and scholars. Foreign nationals from Iran traveling on student and exchange visitor visas would still be able to enter the United States, subject to enhanced screening and vetting requirements. Scholar visas are banned for Iranian foreign nationals per Muslim Ban 3.0. Students and scholars from Somalia would be permitted to come to the United States but be subject to heightened screening. The new rules do not limit travel by visiting students and scholars coming on the appropriate visas from Chad, Libya, and Yemen. However, in banning U.S. entry for business and tourist visas from those three countries, the new restrictions could prevent students and scholars from coming to the United States for short-term visits, such as participating in a conference to present research.

Muslim Ban 3.0, of course, came with its legal challenges. In the state of Hawaii, the U.S. district court judge ruled that Muslim Ban 3.0 "suffers from precisely the same maladies as its predecessor," that "it lacks sufficient findings that the entry of more than 150 million nationals from six specified countries would be 'detrimental to the interests of the United States,'" and that it "plainly discriminates based on nationality" (Wolf & Gomez, 2017, para. 2). In the state of Maryland, new challengers to Muslim Ban 3.0, including the Iranian Students Foundation at the University of Maryland, College Park, joined the fight against it. On October 17, 2017, the U.S. District Court of Maryland ordered a nationwide preliminary injunction against sections of Muslim Ban 3.0 against the designated countries except North Korea and Venezuela. In the Maryland lawsuits challenging the Muslim bans, the district court took note of the harmful roles that Islamophobia and discrimination play in the day-to-day lives of Muslims resulting from the exclusionary measures, as in the following:

> Plaintiffs, John Doe No. 4 states that he "felt insulted" by EO-1 and received "more suspicious looks from people," which caused him to feel that "I am being labeled as a Muslim more often," and that the Proclamation "has made me feel this more strongly" such that "I continue to feel demeaned by the ban." J.R. 461-62. Jane Doe No. 2 states that she understands the Proclamation to fulfill campaign promises to condemn her religion, which has made her feel depressed and has caused her to question whether to remain in the United States because she does not want her children to face discrimination. Afsaneh Khazaeli states that the Proclamation and the predecessor travel bans have made him feel like a "second-class citizen" and has made his family the target of abuse and discrimination. J.R. 465-66. Shapour Shirani states that the anti-Muslim nature of the travel ban has made the separation from his wife "more painful," and the Proclamation has made him "feel even worse" and worry that discrimination against Muslims will persist and interfere with his rights. (*IRAP v. Trump*, D. Md. 2017, p. 33)

It is reasonable to conclude that Muslims generally in the United States, not just the plaintiffs to the Muslim ban litigation, feel condemned, stigmatized, attacked, or discriminated against as a result of the three iterations of the Muslim ban. This materializes in discomfort in Muslims' school, work, and personal lives.

Three days after the district court decisions, the Ninth Circuit Court of Appeals issued a partial stay of Muslim Ban 3.0. This left the preliminary injunction in place only if the citizens of Iran, Chad, Libya, Syria, Yemen, and Somalia could establish that they have "a credible claim of a bona fide relationship with a person or entity in the United States" (*Trump v IRAP*, 20178, p. 12).

In a striking decision made on December 4, 2017, the U.S. Supreme Court stayed the preliminary injunctions issued by U.S. district courts in Hawaii and Maryland, allowing Muslim Ban 3.0 to go into full effect pending a decision from the Supreme Court on the merits. In describing the precedent the Supreme Court set with its decision, Khaled Beydoun (2017b), an associate professor of law at the University of Detroit Mercy, states that this is

> the first time the federal courts, and indeed the Supreme Court, has endorsed this version of the Ban in its entirety. The ruling revives and reinstates the Ban as standing immigration policy. The Supreme Court stay foreshadows a ruling on the constitutional challenges made against the Ban that may allow it to stand for the duration of the Trump administration. (para. 3)

Beydoun further explains:

> The decision is a major victory for Trump's broader Islamophobia campaign, which he mounted as a candidate and now moved forward as president, and a major blow for the more than 100 million Muslims in the six restricted states, and the six to eight million living in the U.S. (Beydoun, 2017b, para. 4)

Finally, in June 2018 the U.S. Supreme Court decided in a 5–4 decision that Muslim Ban 3.0 was a lawful use of the president's executive power and did not violate the First Amendment's Establishment Clause. Although the Supreme Court's decision didn't decide the case on the merits and remanded the case back to the Ninth Circuit Court of Appeals, it did come to the determination that the challenges to the Muslim ban are unlikely to succeed on the merits. In exercising great deference to the president, the majority opinion held that "by its terms, § 1182(f) [of the INA] exudes deference to the President in every clause" (*Trump v. Hawaii*, 2018, s. III, A, para. 2). Completely disregarding the president's Islamophobic statements during his campaign and Muslim ban iterations, the court further determined that the

> President then issued a Proclamation setting forth extensive findings describing how deficiencies in the practices of select foreign governments—several of which are state sponsors of terrorism—deprive the Government of 'sufficient information to assess the risks [those countries' nationals] pose to the United States' (para. 4).

In one of the most inspiring dissenting opinions of our time, Justice Sonia Sotomayor strongly rebutted the majority's assertion that the president acted on sufficient information. Indeed, the September 2017 report cited by the majority was a mere 17 pages (*Hawaii v. Trump*, 2018). The dissent further argued that the "Government's analysis of the vetting practices of hundreds of countries boiled down to such a short document raises serious questions about the legitimacy of the President's proclaimed national-security rationale" (*Trump v. Hawaii*, 2018, s. II, para. 9).

The Supreme Court's majority also used the opportunity to finally—after 75 years—make a pitiful attempt at overturning *Korematsu v. United States*, holding that "*Korematsu* was gravely wrong the day it was decided, has been overruled in the court of history, and—to be clear—'has no place in law under the Constitution'" (*Trump v. Hawaii*, 2018, s. IV, para. 28). However, although overturning *Korematsu*, the Supreme Court's majority opinion ignores the fact that they were perpetuating the blind deference to the president that led the *Korematsu* court astray (Katyal, 2019). Despite overturning *Korematsu*, the court's decision upholding the Muslim ban "merely replace[d] one 'gravely wrong' decision with another" (*Trump v. Hawaii*, 2018, s. IV, para. 5). Specifically, "both courts adopted a posture of broad deference to the executive—even when individual constitutional rights are infringed—when the executive asserts that a policy is necessary to ensure the nation's security" (Katyal, 2019, p. 649). In her dissent, Justice Sotomayor pointed to the disturbing tendency of the court to ignore the blatant Islamophobia that fueled Muslim Ban 3.0. Justice Sotomayor charged the court with betraying the "principle of religious neutrality in the First Amendment" (*Trump v. Hawaii*, 2018, Sotomayor dissent, para. 1) and failing to safeguard it as a fundamental principle. More specifically, she proclaimed that the court's majority "leaves undisturbed a policy first advertised openly and unequivocally as a 'total and complete shutdown of Muslims entering the United States' because the policy now masquerades behind a façade of national-security concerns" (*Trump v. Hawaii*, 2018, Sotomayor dissent, para. 1). Justice Sotomayor's dissent laid bare the court majority's highly abridged account of the facts that ignored the whole record that "paints a far more harrowing picture" (*Trump v. Hawaii*, 2018, Sotomayor dissent, para. 5). Neal Katyal (2019), lead counsel for the state of Hawaii and other plaintiffs in the Supreme court case, summarized what the court got wrong:

> When given the chance to memorialize *Korematsu's* lessons, the court instead made almost every mistake in *Korematsu's* playbook—it accepted the government's arguments at face value, deferred to the executive branch without ensuring that deference was warranted, and confined itself to a narrow review of the Proclamation, examining a "figmentary and artificial" case instead of the one actually before it. (p. 656)

Although meant to overturn *Korematsu*, the Supreme Court's Muslim ban decision for many merely recreated it and strengthened the institutionalized Islamophobia that President Trump's Muslim ban sought to build on. The Supreme Court's rationale was highly criticized and rejected by legal scholars and laypeople alike. If anything, the Supreme Court's Muslim ban decision confirmed the belief for many that the court must adopt a different approach when analyzing and deciding national security cases where they afford a low level of scrutiny and a high level of deference to the executive branch. It encouraged a greater movement to call on the Supreme Court to take not only a less deferential view to national security questions but also a critical view of them—particularly because the court was established to act as a balance of power against the other two branches of government when depriving individuals of their rights.

The Muslim Ban's Effect on Academia and Student Life

Despite repeated recognition from courts and university administrators that Muslim students and faculty make immeasurable contributions to American universities, Muslim students in America continue to lack the support they need to feel comfortable on university campuses. Although universities rallied around the crucial role that Muslims fulfill at U.S. universities, university administrations across the country have routinely failed to make the necessary accommodations to ensure that Muslim students feel safe and comfortable on their campuses. The dissenting opinions in the Hawaii case also noted the detrimental effect this ban has had on higher education in the United States. In Justice Sotomayor's dissent, she argued that the plaintiffs did, in fact, show a likelihood of irreparable harm in the absence of an injunction. She noted:

> Plaintiffs have adduced substantial evidence showing that the Proclamation will result in "a multitude of harms that are not compensable with monetary damages and that are irreparable—among them, prolonged separation from family members, constraints to recruiting and retaining students and faculty members to foster diversity and quality within the University community, and the diminished membership of the [Muslim] Association." (*Trump v. Hawaii*, 2018, Sotomayor dissent, para. 2)

In a separate dissenting opinion, Justice Stephen Breyer argued that failure of the government to engage in the waiver process the way it is defined proves that the waiver process is nothing more than a sham. He argued this is primarily evidenced by the drastic drop in issuance of student visas from the banned countries. More specifically:

> If the Government is not applying the Proclamation's exemption and waiver system, the claim that the Proclamation is a "Muslim ban," rather than a "security-based" ban, becomes much stronger. How could the Government successfully claim that the Proclamation rests on security needs if it is excluding Muslims who satisfy the Proclamation's own terms? At the same time, denying visas to Muslims who meet the Proclamation's own security terms would support the view that the Government excludes them for reasons based upon their religion. (*Trump v. Hawaii*, 2018, Breyer dissent, para. 7)

Justice Breyer cleverly cited Department of State statistics that showed only 258 student visas were issued to applicants from Iran (189), Libya (29), Yemen (40), and Somalia (0) in the first 3 months of 2018. This is less than a quarter of the volume needed to be on track for 2016 student visa levels. In addition, only 40 nonimmigrant visas had been issued to Somali nationals, a decrease of 65% from 2016.

The Chilling Effect: Foreign Nationals

One of the initial direct impacts of the Muslim ban and accompanying Islamophobia perpetuated by the Trump administration has been a decrease in foreign nationals interested in attending university in the United States. "Islamophobic policies, like the Muslim ban, impact far more than immigration or national security policy. Their legal impact is merely one dimension of their aggregate damage" (Beydoun, 2017a, para. 10). Many of the plaintiffs in the Muslim ban litigation, and universities across the country, cited the chilling effect the exclusionary measure will have on students, particularly students seeking higher education opportunities from abroad. University professors and administrators have lamented that they are worried that potential students, in the process of either applying for or accepting admission, will decide not to come to the United States because of the chilling effect (Carapezza, 2017). Although the Trump administration attempted to narrow the scope of the Muslim ban by allowing some student visas to be issued in the present version of the ban for some of the designated countries, it has been made very clear by academics that there will be a residual effect of the Muslim bans' creation of chaos and hardship on those who might otherwise have considered studying in the United States.

According to a survey by the American Association of Collegiate Registrars and Admissions Officers (AACRAO), the number of international students applying to American educational institutions dropped by 40% for fall 2017 (Carapezza, 2017). Not surprisingly, the largest decline came from the Middle East. Researchers also found a dip in applicants from India and China, which currently make up nearly 50% of international student enrollment in the United States (Carapezza, 2017).

The Chilling Effect: Academic Freedom

The negative impact of the bans reaches more than just international students seeking an education in the United States—it also results in negative effects on Muslim students at college campuses across the nation, regardless of their immigration status. In 2016, the American Association of University Professors (AAUP) set forth some of the expected assaults on academic freedom from the then president-elect's proposed exclusionary measures against Muslims in a released statement:

> Trump's campaign has already threatened academic freedom. His remarks about minorities, immigrants, and women have on some campuses had a

chilling effect on the rights of students and faculty members to speak out. At some events Trump held on university campuses, students who opposed him said they were harassed or threatened. His call for an "ideological screening test" for admission to the United States could make it difficult for universities to attract students and scholars from other countries and to engage in the international exchange of ideas so vital to academic freedom. (American Association of University Professors, 2016, para. 2)

As a result of the Trump effect, discriminatory incidents against religious minorities have become increasingly common at American college campuses. Muslim students are particularly vulnerable to being a target of one these incidents (Bishop, 2015). And although the AAUP is correct about the negative effects these exclusionary policies will have on college students, the targeting of Muslim college students and criminalization of them is nothing new. The New York Police Department infamously used informants to infiltrate Muslim student groups on college campuses and collected the names, phone numbers, and addresses of those who attended (Apuzzo & Goldstein, 2014). In 2016, an FBI presentation published by *The Intercept* revealed that the FBI was conditioning its agents to look for informants in mosques and Muslim Student Associations (MSAs) (Currier, 2016b). The FBI documents state that agents searched Facebook "to find individuals who are dramatically increasing their levels of piety—that's the demographic you want. . . . Since we're looking for young people re-engaging with their Islamic faith" (Currier, 2016a, para. 2). It continues, "the local MSA is a great place to start" (para. 6). Ramzi Kassem, a law professor at the City University of New York who directs an initiative that works with those targeted by counterterrorism policies, stated that the "FBI's focus on Muslim student groups does not make anyone safer," and that the use of these tactics "comes at the expense of students whose college experience is no longer a time for intellectual exploration and the building of lasting friendships but a paranoid nightmare where certain thoughts are taboo and your classmate might be an informant" (as quoted in Currier, 2016a, para. 10).

The Increase of Islamophobia and the Radical Right on College Campuses

The president and his advisers and representatives sought to support their attempts to enact discriminatory laws against Muslims, such as the Muslim bans, through a flood of highly publicized Islamophobic statements, which were featured repeatedly on daily news cycles. This led directly to an image, in mainstream media and culture, of Muslims as inherently dangerous, untrustworthy, and violent. As a result of this newly commonplace and accepted Islamophobic discourse, Muslims have been depicted as un-American. On college campuses across the nation, activists, students, and faculty, dismayed by these depictions, have rightfully feared the impact the Muslim bans, and the discussions surrounding them, would have on Muslim American student life. As will be discussed, despite recognition that students are being increasingly exposed to these harmful views and that Muslim students will be particularly impacted, university administrations have largely failed to take necessary precautions to defend their Muslim students.

In California, Muslim college students across the state have long stressed that they face a campus climate hostile toward Muslims. In October 2012 the University of California (UC) commissioned a committee to look at the campus climate for Arabs and Muslims, with a separate committee focusing on Jewish students. This was mainly in response to the Irvine 11, where 11 Muslim students from the UC, Irvine, were criminally prosecuted for their nonviolent protest on campus of then Israeli ambassador Michael Oren. Many Muslim students on UC campuses during and after the convictions of the Irvine 11 argued that Muslim students are treated unfairly and that the UC system does not do enough to proactively counter Islamophobia on its campuses. The UC Campus Climate project fact-finding team for Muslim and Arab students noted that during the 2012 investigation "almost every Muslim or Arab student the Team encountered shared frustration and even pain with prejudicial experiences on a UC campus, which they believed were due to their Muslim or Arab identity or the expression of their identity" (Turk, Senzaki, Howard, & Rowther, 2012, p. 5). More specifically, the fact-finding team noted, "Muslim and Arab students operate within a climate of suspicion and mistrust on UC campuses and feel selectively scrutinized and harassed, particularly in the functioning of student organization activities and events" (Turk et al., 2012, p. 6). In terms of on-campus harassment, the fact-finding team found that at UCLA, UC Berkeley, and UC Davis, students reported harassment primarily from other students and that a majority of these situations involved anti-Muslim, bigoted comments, and identity bashing from other students. "Visibly Muslim students, particularly women who observe hijab and wear religious headscarves, encounter frequent bigoted comments" (p. 5). In the present it is easy to see how the 2012 Campus Climate fact-finding conclusions illustrate that the Trump presidency and his repeated attempts at declaring Muslim bans as a necessary security measure to target a threat within our society has confounded the already fragile campus climate for Muslim students.

After the damage from the election, many college campuses committed to surveying their students on how they perceived campus environments and generating subsequent campus climate reports. Several reports noted that Muslim students were less likely to report feeling welcomed, respected, and like they belonged and were more likely to report feeling excluded (Campana, Kalsow, McChesney, & Zhiang, 2017; Richmond, 2017). One campus climate report stated that survey respondents reported an atmosphere of "unfriendliness" toward Muslims (Bolt, 2017). Another report noted that Muslim student respondents were more likely to report a negative campus climate and perceive the overall institutional climate as religiously intolerant (University of Chicago, 2017). The University of Chicago's 2016 campus climate report findings noted that members of their campus community who identify as Muslim were most likely to report nonphysical discrimination and/or harassment and online discrimination and/or harassment (University of Chicago, 2017). The report also disclosed that approximately 41% of respondents who identify as Muslim have avoided disclosing or concealed their religious identity due to fear of negative consequences or harassment from a peer, and approximately 46% of Muslim respondents report having concealed their support for those of their religious identity due to fear of intimidation or harassment from a peer (University of Chicago, 2017).

Far-right groups focused on promoting Islamophobia and disparaging Islam are taking advantage of the fragile campus climate toward Muslims. The Southern Poverty Law Center (SPLC) has stated that after the Trump election, the bigoted alternative right, or alt-right, movement gained traction at college campuses across the country. Sponsored by alt-right groups on college campuses,

> extremist speakers are touring colleges and universities across the country to recruit students to their brand of bigotry, often igniting protests and making national headlines. Their appearances have inspired a fierce debate over free speech and the direction of the country. (Southern Poverty Law Center, 2017, para. 1)

For example, one group responsible for much of the Islamophobic propaganda spreading at college campuses across the country is David Horowitz's "Freedom Center," which is described by SPLC as a hate organization that is "the premier financier of anti-Muslim voices and radical ideologies" and "exporter of misinformation" (Schmidt, 2016, para. 1). Horowitz is known as "a prominent figure instrumental in demonizing Islam and spreading fear about an Islamic takeover of Western society" (Dajani, 2017, para. 1). Specifically, the Freedom Center is responsible for publishing and distributing posters with negative depictions of Muslim or Arab students and faculty as a way to vilify Muslims and critics of Israel's human rights violations against the Palestinians. The objective of the defamatory posters is to subject the targeted students and faculty to verbal, physical, and psychological harassment. The posters used by the Freedom Center in their Islamophobia campaign on college campuses are reminiscent of Nazi propaganda posters used to vilify Jews during World War II. Although many college students and faculty trusted their university's strong condemnation of such defamatory and hate-filled propaganda on campus, the actual responses from many university administrators were disappointing. For example, posters from the Freedom Center were seen across the San Francisco State University campus. The posters falsely identified faculty and students as "Terrorist Supporters" (Figure 1.1). Subsequently, the president of the university, Les Wong, provided no condemnation of the posters and even refused to have the posters removed, claiming them to be legitimate free speech instruments (Dajani,

Figure 1.1. Posters from the Freedom Center posted across the San Francisco State University campus. The posters falsely identified faculty and students as "terrorist supporters."

2017). Many argue, and rightly so, that such inaction and defense of defamatory posters as "free speech" is tantamount to endorsing them.

After the announcement of the coming of a second executive order for a Muslim ban by President Trump in February 2017, a wave of offensive posters was reported at multiple universities across the country (Stone, 2017). In February 2017, the alt-right organization American Vanguard, purporting to "want to be at the forefront of the reawakening of the white racial consciousness" consisting of "young white Americans defending [their] race and nation against all enemies, foreign and domestic" (quoted in Stone, 2017, paras. 10–11), conducted a poster campaign. The hate organization, according to their website, organized a mass poster effort to display their hate materials at Texas State University, Rice University, the University of North Texas, the University of Texas at Dallas, Collin College, Abilene Christian University,

Figure 1.2. Alt-right organization American Vanguard's poster displaying hate materials such as this poster that states, "Imagine a Muslim-Free America."

and Louisiana State University. The posters also made appearances at Rutgers University and University of Texas at Austin. The posters contained imagery of the World Trade Center's twin towers that were attacked on 9/11 and language asking the reader to "Imagine a Muslim-Free America" (Figure 1.2).

It was reported that posters targeting Muslims had appeared on the UC San Diego campus. These posters imitated the shameful poster announcements for the internment of Japanese Americans during World War II (see Figure 1.3). The anonymous creator of the posters at UC San Diego, which called for the evacuation of Muslims in San Diego by April 8, 2018, clarified that the intention behind the poster was to stir "shock and anger" over the proposed Muslim bans and wanted them to be a "warning presented as a possible future" (Constante, 2017, para. 4). However, the poster's creator, regardless of the intention, ignored the imminent fear that Muslim students,

Figure 1.3. Posters targeting Muslims appeared at the UC San Diego campus. The posters were designed to imitate announcements for the internment of Japanese Americans during World War II.

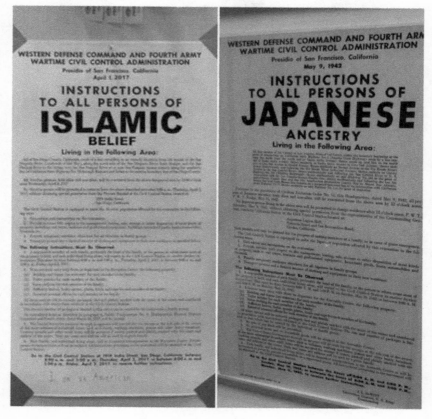

and other students coming from a history of Japanese internment, felt after viewing the posters.

Many Muslim students have argued that since President Trump's election and the Muslim bans, universities have been going out of their way to accommodate Islamophobes going to college campuses, rather than doing everything in their power to protect the vulnerable students that they target. Indeed, at UC Berkeley, the Berkeley College Republicans invited several alt-right speakers such as David Horowitz, and the campus newspaper, *The Daily Cal*, reported that the university administration "doesn't just allow them to plan the event. It's bending over backwards, bleeding resources to ensure they happen" (Editorial Board, 2017, para. 3). At Stanford University, the Muslim Student Union and a coalition of other student organizations in an open letter condemned an event hosted by the Stanford College Republicans inviting Robert Spencer, whom the SPLC described as an anti-Muslim propagandist. Spencer is the director of the Muslim-bashing website Jihad Watch and the cofounder of Stop Islamization of America and the American Freedom Defense Initiative, both of which are classified as hate groups by the SPLC. The open letter noted that Islamophobia is not only institutionalized in U.S. foreign policy and immigration policy with Trump's xenophobic Muslim ban but also now institutionalizing itself on college campuses by legitimizing speakers such as Spencer at the expense of associated student funds and "endorsing Spencer's bigotry with Stanford's name and students' money" (Stanford Coalition of Concerned Students, 2017, para. 3).

While American university campuses are becoming playgrounds and platforms for mainstream Islamophobes like Horowitz and Spencer, it is safe to say that the campus climate for Muslim students will continue to deteriorate. The guises of free speech that universities are hiding behind help to create the pathway for more discrimination, intolerance, and marginalization of Muslim college students.

Discussion Questions

1. Does Trump's Muslim ban fit into a larger pattern in U.S. history as it relates to exclusion or immigration?
2. Have you seen a change on your college campus after the Muslim ban? If yes, has it been positive or negative?
3. Do you understand the last iteration of the ban, as written by President Trump, to be discriminatory or superficially neutral? Are Trump's extrinsic comments relevant to any discussion of discriminatory intent of the ban?
4. In what ways might the Muslim ban lead to increased alienation of Muslims in the United States?

References

Almasy, S., & Simon, D. (2017, March 30). A timeline of President Trump's travel bans. *CNN*. Retrieved from https://www.cnn.com/2017/02/10/us/trump-travel-ban-timeline/index.html

American Association of University Professors. (2016, November 9). *Higher education after the 2016 election*. Retrieved from https://www.aaup.org/news/higher-education-after-2016-election#.WrBZ-ajwaUl

Apuzzo, M., & Goldstein, J. (2014, April 15). New York drops unit that spied on Muslims. *New York Times*. Retrieved from https://www.nytimes.com/2014/04/16/nyregion/police-unit-that-spied-on-muslims-is-disbanded.html

Beydoun, K. (2017a, May 7). How Muslim ban incites vigilante Islamophobic violence. *Al-Jazeera*. Retrieved from https://www.aljazeera.com/indepth/opinion/2017/03/muslim-ban-incites-vigilante-islamophobic-violence-170307065614706.html

Beydoun, K. (2017b, December 6). The US Supreme Court has empowered Trump's Islamophobia. *Al-Jazeera*. Retrieved from https://www.aljazeera.com/indepth/opinion/supreme-court-empowered-trump-islamophobia-171206113208307.html

Bishop, T. (2015, November 5). Being Muslim on campus. *Atlantic*. Retrieved from https://www.theatlantic.com/politics/archive/2015/11/muslim-students-university/416994/

Bolt, J. (2017, February 17). "Climate Survey" shows general feeling of safety, but acknowledges issues. *WVU Today*. Retrieved from https://wvutoday.wvu.edu/stories/2017/02/17/-climate-survey-shows-general-feeling-of-safety-but-acknowledges-issues

Bromwich, J. (2016, November 17). Trump camp's talk of registry and Japanese internment raises Muslims' fears. *New York Times*. Retrieved from https://www.nytimes.com/2016/11/18/us/politics/japanese-internment-muslim-registry.html

Campana, K., Kalsow, S., McChesney, J., & Zhiang, M. (2017). *Campus climate survey 2017*. Retrieved from https://www.mnsu.edu/cultdiv/climate_study_report_final_1.pdf

Carapezza, K. (2017, April 17). Travel ban's "chilling effect" could cost universities hundreds of millions. *NPR*. Retrieved from https://www.npr.org/sections/ed/2017/04/07/522773429/travel-bans-chilling-effect-could-cost-universities-hundreds-of-millions

Chehata, F. (2018, January). *We won't be banned: Fighting the 2017 Muslim bans*. Retrieved from https://ca.cair.com/downloads/Muslim_Ban_Final.pdf

Constante, A. (2017). Student who created Muslim "internment notice" poster responds to outrage. *NBC News*. Retrieved from https://www.nbcnews.com/news/asian-america/student-who-created-muslim-internment-notice-posters-responds-outrage-n729156

Council on American-Islamic Relations (CAIR). (2017, July 17). *CAIR report shows 2017 on track to becoming one of the worst years ever for anti-Muslim hate crimes* [Press release]. Retrieved from https://www.cair.com/press-center/press-releases/14476-cair-report-shows-2017-on-track-to-becoming-one-of-worst-years-ever-for-anti-muslim-hate-crimes.html

Currier, C. (2016a, September 29). *The FBI wanted to target Yemenis through student groups and mosques.* Retrieved from https://theintercept.com/2016/09/29/the-fbi-wanted-to-target-yemenis-through-student-groups-and-mosques/

Currier, C. (2016b, October, 17). *Muslim students speak out against FBI informant plan exposed by the* Intercept. Retrieved from https://theintercept.com/2016/10/17/muslim-students-speak-out-against-fbi-informant-plan-exposed-by-the-intercept/

Dajani, J. (2017, September 24). Islamophobia at home at San Francisco State University. *Huffington Post.* Retrieved from https://www.huffingtonpost.com/entry/islamophobia-at-home-at-san-francisco-state-university_us_59c83c0be4b0b7022a646bb0

Editorial Board. (2017, September 22). Right-wing student groups invite bigoted trolls to invade campus under guise of free speech. *Daily Cal.* Retrieved from https://www.dailycal.org/2017/09/22/right-wing-student-groups-invite-bigoted-trolls-invade-campus-guise-free-speech/

Executive Order No. 13,769, 82 Fed. Reg. 8977 (2017).

Executive Order No. 13,780, 82 Fed. Reg. 13209 (2017).

Flores, R. (2016, November 17). Kris Kobach says Trump team considering a Muslim registry. *CBS News.* Retrieved from https://www.cbsnews.com/news/kris-kobach-says-trump-team-considering-a-muslim-registry/

Hauslohner, A., & Johnson, J. (2017, May 20). "I think Islam hates us": A timeline of Trump's comments about Islam and Muslims. *Washington Post.* Retrieved from https://www.washingtonpost.com/news/post-politics/wp/2017/05/20/i-think-islam-hates-us-a-timeline-of-trumps-comments-about-islam-and-muslims/?utm_term=.0e356f8b02ac

Hawaii v. Trump, 241 F. Supp.3d 1119, 1129 (9th Cir. 2017).

International Refugee Assistance Project (IRAP) v. Trump, 241 F. Supp.3d 539 (D. Md. 2017).

International Refugee Assistance Project (IRAP) v. Trump, 857 F.3d 554 (4th Cir. 2017).

Jackson, B. (2004). Documentation of international students in the United States: Forging alliances or fostering alienation? *Georgetown Immigration Law Journal, 18,* 373–394.

Johnson, J. (2015, December 7). Trump calls for "total and complete shutdown of Muslims entering the United States." *Washington Post.* Retrieved from https://www.washingtonpost.com/news/post-politics/wp/2015/12/07/donald-trump-calls-for-total-and-complete-shutdown-of-muslims-entering-the-united-states/

Kanowitz, S. (2017, May 5). Trump's travel ban may have chilling effect on international student enrollment. *Washington Diplomat.* Retrieved from http://www.washdiplomat.com/index.php?option=com_content&view=article&id=15350:t

rumps-travel-ban-may-have-chilling-effect-on-international-student-enrollment
&catid=1557&Itemid=428

Katyal, N. (2019). *Trump v. Hawaii*: How the Supreme Court simultaneously overturned and revived Korematsu. *Yale Law Journal Forum, 128*, 641–656.

Levinson-Waldman, R., & Patel, F. (2017). *The Islamophobic administration.* Retrieved from https://www.brennancenter.org/sites/default/files/publications/ BCJ_Islamophobic_Administration.pdf

Liptak, A. (2017). Trump refugee restrictions allowed for now; Ban on grandparents is rejected. *New York Times.* Retrieved from https://www.nytimes.com/2017/07/19/ us/politics/trump-travel-ban-supreme-court.html

Middle East Studies Association (MESA). (2017). *About MESA* (Mission Statement). Retrieved from http://mesana.org/about/index.html

Patel, F., & Price, M. (2016, November 22). *Muslim registry or NSEERS reboot would be unconstitutional.* Retrieved from https://www.brennancenter.org/blog/muslim-registry-or-nseers-reboot-would-be-unconstitutional

Pew Research Center. (2017, July 26). *U.S. Muslims concerned about their place in society, but continue to believe in the American dream.* Retrieved from http://www .pewforum.org/2017/07/26/findings-from-pew-research-centers-2017-survey-of-us-muslims/

Redden, E. (2017, September 26). Travel ban 3.0. *Inside Higher Education.* Retrieved from https://www.insidehighered.com/news/2017/09/26/new-travel-restrictions-raise-questions-concerns-higher-ed

Registration of Certain Nonimmigrant Aliens From Designated Countries (2002, December 18). 67 Fed. Reg. 77,136, 77,136 (December 18, 2002). Retrieved from https://www.gpo.gov/fdsys/pkg/FR-2002-12-18/pdf/02-32045.pdf

Removing Designated Countries From the National Security Entry-Exit Registration System (NSEERS). (April 28, 2011). 76 Fed. Reg. 23,830, 23,831 to be codified at 8 CFR 264.1. Retrieved from https://www.gpo.gov/fdsys/pkg/FR-2011-04- 28/pdf/2011-10305.pdf

Richmond, T. (2017, November 1). UW survey: Fewer underrepresented students feel welcome. *The Seattle Times.* Retrieved from https://www.seattletimes.com/ nation-world/uw-madison-survey-fewer-minority-students-feel-welcome/

Schemo, D. (2001, November 18). Eager for foreign students, universities persuade senator to drop plan to limit visas. *New York Times.* Retrieved from http://www .nytimes.com/2001/11/18/us/nation-challenged-students-eager-for-foreign-students-universities-persuade.html

Schmidt, K. (2016, October 21). SPLC-named hate group calls students "terrorists" in campus posters. *Tufts Daily.* Retrieved from https://tuftsdaily.com/ news/2016/10/21/students-named-as-terrorists-in-campus-posters-by-horowitz-center/

Southern Poverty Law Center. (2017, August 10). *The alt-right on campus: What students need to know.* Retrieved from https://www.splcenter.org/20170810/alt-right-campus-what-students-need-know#alt-right-targeting

Stanford Coalition of Concerned Students. (2017, November 8). An open letter to the College Republicans regarding Robert Spencer. *Stanford Daily*. Retrieved from https://www.stanforddaily.com/2017/11/08/an-open-letter-to-the-college-republicans-regarding-robert-spencer/

State of Hawaii v. Trump, 263 F. Supp.3d 1049 (D. Ha. 2017).

Stone, B. (2017, February 15). Muslim-free America posters turn up on multiple college campuses. *USA Today*. Retrieved from https://www.usatoday.com/story/college/2017/02/15/muslim-free-america-posters-turn-up-on-multiple-college-campuses/37427599/

Stuart, T. (2017, March 6). Everything that's different in the new Trump travel ban. *Rolling Stone*. Retrieved from https://www.rollingstone.com/politics/features/everything-thats-different-in-the-new-trump-travel-ban-w470623

Torbati, Y. (2017, April 27). Number of U.S. visas to citizens of Trump travel ban nations drops. *Reuters*. Retrieved from http://www.reuters.com/article/us-usa-immigration-visasanalysis/number-of-u-s-visas-to-citizens-of-trump-travel-ban-nations-drops-idUSKBN17T34G

Trump v. Hawaii, 585 U.S. ____ (2018) (Sotomayor, dissenting).

Trump v. Hawaii, 585 U.S. ____(2018) (Breyer, dissenting).

Trump v. Hawaii, 585 U.S. ____ (2018).

Trump v. International Refugee Assistant Project, 582 U.S. ____ (2017).

Turk, J., Senzaki, N., Howard, T., & Rowther, A. (2012). *Muslim & Arab student campus climate at the University of California fact-finding team report & recommendations*. Retrieved from https://cascholars4academicfreedom.files.wordpress.com/2012/07/muslim-arab-student-climate-report-final.pdf

University of Chicago. (2017, April). *Spring 2016 campus climate survey, religion and spirituality*. Retrieved from https://provost.uchicago.edu/sites/default/files/documents/reports/ClimateSurveyReport.ReligionSpirituality.pdf

Washington v. Trump, 2017 WL 462040 (W.D. Wash. 2017).

Washington v. Trump, 847 F. 3d 1151, 1159 (9th Cir. 2017).

Wolf, R., & Gomez, A. (2017, October 17). Federal judge in Hawaii blocks Trump's third travel ban. *USA Today*. Retrieved from https://www.usatoday.com/story/news/politics/2017/10/17/federal-judge-hawaii-strikes-down-trumps-third-travel-ban/773074001/

Zapotosky, M. (2017, February 22). A new travel ban with "mostly minor technical differences"? That probably won't cut it, analysts say. *Washington Post*. Retrieved from https://www.washingtonpost.com/world/national-security/a-new-travel-ban-with-mostly-minor-technical-differences-that-probably-wont-cut-it-analysts-say/2017/02/22/8ae9d7e6-f918-11e6-bf01-d47f8cf9b643_story.html?utm_term=.0172880bea55

2

CRIMINALIZATION OF MUSLIM STUDENTS POST-9/11

Parwana Anwar

September 11, 2001, marked the single most horrific terrorist attack on U.S. soil, with 2,726 people losing their lives (Centers for Disease Control and Prevention, 2002). The aftermath of this attack shifted the focus of various law enforcement agencies to Muslims and Arabs. Agencies such as the Federal Bureau of Investigation (FBI), Immigration and Customs Enforcement (ICE), and New York Police Department (NYPD) began to actively and relentlessly monitor the activities of these community members. In 2011, the Associated Press released a Pulitzer Prize–winning months-long series outlining the NYPD's surveillance of minority and particularly Muslim neighborhoods since the 9/11 terror attacks (Associated Press, 2012). NYPD, with help from the Central Intelligence Agency (CIA), established the secret Demographics Unit, later renamed the Zone Assessment Unit, which assembled databases on where Muslims lived, worked, and prayed. Police infiltrated Muslim student groups; placed informants—known as *mosque crawlers*—in mosques to monitor sermons with no evidence of wrongdoing; and catalogued every Muslim in New York who adopted new, Americanized surnames (Goldman & Apuzzo, 2012). This chapter will focus on how law enforcement, including the FBI, CIA, and police agencies, have used a variety of methods to spy on and monitor Muslim communities without any suspicion of wrongdoing. It will discuss the cases of Mostafa Tabatabainejad, the Irvine 11, and Clock Boy as three examples of how Muslims have been criminalized. This chapter will address the ongoing surveillance of Muslim students and the negative impact of targeting Muslims. The chapter will conclude with a set of recommendations and provide discussion questions to further engage this topic.

Surveillance of Muslims

In its report titled *Factsheet: The NYPD Muslim Surveillance Program*, the American Civil Liberties Union (ACLU; 2017) details that since at least 2002, the NYPD Intelligence Division has engaged in suspicionless surveillance of Muslims in New York City and beyond. NYPD's Intelligence Division units engaged in the Muslim surveillance program include the Demographics Unit; the Cyber Intelligence Unit; the Intelligence Analysis Unit; and the Terrorist Interdiction Unit (ACLU, 2017). The report concludes that the NYPD's Intelligence Division has

> singled out Muslim religious and community leaders, mosques, student associations, organizations, businesses, and individuals for pervasive surveillance that is discriminatory and not conducted against institutions or individuals belonging to any other religious faith, or the public at large. The NYPD's surveillance program is based on a false and unconstitutional premise: that Muslim religious belief and practices are a basis for law enforcement scrutiny. (ACLU, 2017, p. 1)

Law enforcement around the country, including the FBI and police agencies, uses a variety of methods to spy on and monitor Muslim communities without any suspicion of wrongdoing. The NYPD was notorious for using plainclothes officers—called "rakers"—and deploying them to Muslim communities where they could blend in "consistent with their ethnicity and/or language" (ACLU, 2017, p. 1). They aimed to compile information on the community, listen in on conversations at Muslim restaurants and businesses, and identify Muslim "hotspots"—hence the term *rakers*, as in "raking the coals" (ACLU, 2017, p. 2). With the recruitment of the previously mentioned mosque crawlers to act as inside observers, the NYPD also used a method termed *create and capture*, which "instructed informants to 'create' conversations about jihad or terrorism to 'capture' and report the responses to the police. Informants are often selected from a pool of arrestees, prisoners, or suspects who are pressured into becoming informants" (ACLU, 2017, p. 2).

In his 2013 report in the *Guardian*, "The FBI's Anticipatory Prosecution of Muslims to Criminalize Speech," Glenn Greenwald details that since 9/11, U.S. Muslims have been routinely targeted with this same tactic of preemptive prosecution, designed to take people engaged in religious and political advocacy disliked by the U.S. government—usually very young, impressionable Muslims with no criminal history—and use paid informants to trick them into saying just enough to turn them into criminals who are then prosecuted and imprisoned. This pattern then repeats itself over and over. Greenwald (2013) writes:

> The FBI ensnares some random Muslim in a garden-variety criminal investigation involving financial fraud or drugs. Rather than prosecute him, the FBI puts the Muslim criminal suspect on its payroll, sending him into Muslim communities and mosques in order not only to spy on American Muslims, but to befriend them and then actively manipulate them into saying just enough to make their prosecution possible. At times, the FBI's informants have been so unstable and aggressive in trying to recruit members to join Terrorist plots that the targeted mosque members themselves have reported the informant to the FBI. (para. 4)

At the direction of these paid informants, who know that their ongoing payments depend on assisting prosecutions, young Muslims in their late teens or early twenties end up saying something hostile or politically offensive about the United States. The Department of Justice takes those inflammatory political statements and combines them with evidence of a commitment to the religion of Islam to paint a picture of a dangerous jihadist. Federal judges, notorious for subservience to the government in cases involving terrorism and Muslims, allow the introduction of dubious government evidence against these defendants. Greenwald (2013) asserts,

> Prosecutors use this combination to convince a jury of Americans—inculcated with more than a decade of intense Islamophobic propaganda—to convict the defendants under "material support for terrorism" statutes even though they have harmed nobody and have taken no real steps toward doing so. The case is based overwhelmingly on the political and religious beliefs of the defendants, which are enough to convince American jurors that they are Bad People. These convictions not only result in decades of prison, but incarceration in special facilities reserved mostly for Muslims that, in most respects, are as restrictive and oppressive as those found at Guantanamo. (para. 6)

To catch criminal behavior in the absence of a plan requires the criminalization of previously legal behavior, surveillance tactics to determine who the "pre-criminals" are, and a way to identify these people. Since 9/11, half of the terrorism prosecutions have involved informants, and more than a quarter have used government sting operations. In some cases, the government has not only provided all the materials from beginning to end but also manufactured the plot (Stahl & Theoharis, 2017).

After years of denying the existence of the Demographics Unit, NYPD ultimately acknowledged it and said that they hoped the unit would serve as an early warning system for terrorism. However, in more than six years of spying on Muslim neighborhoods, eavesdropping on conversations, and cataloguing mosques, Assistant Chief Thomas Galati admitted in an unsealed deposition that the NYPD's secret Demographics Unit never generated a lead or triggered a terrorism investigation (Goldman & Apuzzo, 2012).

It is this unconstitutional bias against Muslims that has pervaded society since 9/11 and has made them the target of unwarranted police scrutiny around the country. This discriminatory belief system and unwarranted preventive prosecution against Muslims as a whole serve as the backdrop to the disparate treatment and criminalization of Muslim students seen in high schools and college campuses across the nation today.

In the years following 9/11, young Muslims, South Asians, Hindus, Sikhs, and Arabs have reported that they often feel unsafe and unwelcome in their schools because of harassment and bullying related to their faith, national origin, or immigration status. According to *Growing in Faith*, a report from the Council on American-Islamic Relations (CAIR, 2013), 50% of American Muslim students in California reported "being subjected to mean comments and rumors about them because of their religion" (p. 10). And it is not always Muslims or Arabs who have been harassed as terrorists. A 2014 report published by the Sikh Coalition entitled *Go Home Terrorist* found that more than 50% of Sikh students reported being bullied, although their religion is completely distinct from Islam. The number rose to 67% for Sikh youth who wear turbans or *dastars* (Sikh Coalition, 2014). Cases involving Muslims such as Mostafa Tabatabainejad, the Irvine 11, and Clock Boy are three examples of how Muslims have been targeted and criminalized.

Mostafa Tabatabainejad

Mostafa Tabatabainejad was an Iranian American Muslim and fourth-year University of California, Los Angeles, student. His case is one egregious example of the disparate treatment experienced by Muslim students on college campuses since 9/11. On November 14, 2006, Tabatabainejad was entering Powell Library on the campus of UCLA to study during finals week. The police were called after Tabatabainejad refused to provide his BruinCard (student ID) to a UCLA community service officer (i.e. student volunteer). Asking students to show ID was not a routine practice, and Tabatabainejad felt he was being singled out because of his Middle Eastern ethnicity. For this reason, he refused to show his ID and instead asked the community service officer if he had asked anyone else that evening to show their ID. The community service officer threatened to call campus police if he did not show his ID. Tabatabainejad, being confident the campus police would take his side as he felt he was being harassed, invited the community service officer to do so. When the campus police arrived they did not ask questions and, instead, immediately handcuffed Tabatabainejad with plastic wrist restraints and physically attempted to remove him from the library. Police tasered him at least five times, although Tabatabainejad said repeatedly he would leave ("UCLA Taser Incident," n.d.).

A painful six-minute video of this incident has widely circulated online and Tabatabainejad can be heard screaming, "I have a medical condition!" while his hands are bound behind his back. Students had gathered around and watched the incident unfold. People can be heard screaming for the officers to stop. A male voice can be heard telling officers he wants their badge numbers. A female yells, "STOP! It's so wrong!" Although a Taser inflicts serious pain and stuns the individual, officers were giving him no time to recover from the blast before commanding him to stand up and threatening to taser him again (Turbanhead, 2006).

Discharging a Taser is usually very high on the use of force scale with which law enforcement are trained. Normally, officers are trained to use Tasers when they are in physical fear for their safety and/or are with combative and violent individuals and suspects. After an in-depth investigation into the incident, UCLA police were told to limit the use of Tasers to violent or aggressive people and to bar the use of the device on people who are passively resistant or handcuffed (Bobb, Barge, & Naguib, 2007). Tabatabainejad filed a federal lawsuit alleging that the officers used excessive force and violated the Americans with Disabilities Act. The case was settled on May 15, 2009, with UCLA agreeing to pay $220,000 for Tabatabainejad's medical and legal fees.

The Irvine 11

On February 8, 2010, Israeli Ambassador Michael Oren was a featured speaker on the University of California, Irvine (UCI), campus. During his speech, several Muslim students stood up one at a time and interrupted him, shouting complaints about Israel. When the repeated outbursts continued deep into Oren's speech, the ambassador huddled with his security aides to decide whether to continue speaking. He did continue, but by the time the speech was over, 11 Muslim students had been arrested. The group became known as the "Irvine 11," although 3 were students from the University of California, Riverside (UCR) (Medina, 2011).

In the wake of the event, the chief executive of the Jewish Federation of Orange County, Shalom Elcott, put UCI on notice, stating the Jewish community would intensely monitor the response of the university. "While it's nice to condemn hate speech in general, we expect a very specific response from the University of California leadership based on what transpired in that room," Elcott said. In addition to prosecuting the students "to the fullest extent of the law," Elcott said he expected future activities of the Muslim Students Union to be closely scrutinized and would like to see their programming stripped of public funding (quoted in Harris, 2010, para. 4). Hillel president Wayne Firestone joined the Orange County federation in its call for a harsh reaction from the university. Firestone stated, "I do believe that strong disciplinary procedures by the university, whether or not they're prosecuted criminally, is in order here" (quoted in Harris, 2010, para. 7).

Additionally, the Zionist Organization of America (ZOA) called for donors to stop supporting UCI and for Jewish students not to apply there. A ZOA statement accused the university of enabling bigotry and violating civil rights "by failing to condemn long-standing anti-Semitic and Israel-bashing speech and conduct on campus, and failing to enforce its own policies against the perpetrators" (Harris, 2010, para. 8).

In response, Orange County District Attorney Tony Rackauckus filed the following misdemeanor charges against the students: Penal Code section 403, disturbance of a meeting, and Penal Code section 182/403, conspiracy to disturb a meeting. In a statement, Rackauckus said, "This case is being filed because there was an organized attempt to squelch the speaker, who was invited to speak to a group at UCI." Rackauckus's statement continued:

> These defendants meant to stop this speech and stop anyone else from hearing his ideas, and they did so by disrupting a lawful meeting. This is a clear violation of the law and failing to bring charges against this conduct would amount to a failure to uphold the Constitution. (Jolly, Galvin, & Hernandez, 2011, para. 4)

A prosecutor must prove the following elements to convict a defendant of disturbing a public meeting:

1. The defendant intentionally committed acts that violated implicit customs or explicit rules for governing a public meeting.
2. The defendant knew or reasonably should have known that his or her acts violated those customs or rules.
3. The defendant's acts substantially and unlawfully interfered with the conduct of the meeting.

A person is not guilty of the crime unless the defendant's acts themselves, and not the message or expressive content of the acts, substantially interfered with the conduct of the meeting. . . . When deciding whether the defendant knew or reasonably should have known that (his/her) acts violated the (implicit customs or usages of/[or] explicit rules for governing) the meeting, you may consider whether someone warned or requested the defendant to stop (his/her) activities. (Disturbing a Public Meeting, 1872/1994)

Penal Code 403 is a misdemeanor in California law. As such, it carries a maximum sentence of up to six months in county jail. However, judges have discretion to grant probation with little or no actual jail time. The exact sentence in a given case depends on the circumstances of the offense and the defendant's prior criminal record, if any.

In glaring contrast to the Jewish Federation of Orange County and ZOA, 30 University of California Jewish Studies faculty members asked the Orange County district attorney to drop the criminal charges against the 11 Muslim students. The faculty members, from 7 University of California campuses, were the second Jewish group to come out in support of the students. The Jewish Voice for Peace organization also supported dropping charges against the students (Fishkoff, 2011). In a letter, the 30 members of the Jewish Studies departments said they disagreed with the students' actions, but did not believe "such peaceful protest" (para. 4) should be criminally prosecuted. They also noted that the students and the Muslim Student Union already had been punished by the UCI and called those sanctions "sufficient" (para. 4).

Jewish Voice for Peace, an Oakland-based group that's often at odds with Israeli policy toward Palestinians, gave the Orange County district attorney a petition signed by more than 5,000 people in support of the 11 Muslim students. Rachel Roberts was among the group's members delivering the petition to the district attorney's office in Santa Ana. She said the criminal charges went too far. "They left as soon as they were asked to leave. They were escorted out by police and campus security," Roberts said. She continued, "And they didn't intend to rush the stage. They didn't intend to take over the space. They simply stood up to make a statement in a way that they had no other way of making. And then they left" (Valot, 2011, paras. 4–5).

Roberts stated a few months prior to the UCI incident that Jewish Voice for Peace did what the Muslim students did. She said they disrupted a speech by Israeli prime minister Benjamin Netanyahu in New Orleans, but no one was arrested. Roberts stated,

> We did exactly what the Irvine kids did. We criticized Israeli policy. . . . We did it as part of like a popcorn action with one person disrupting, then another person disrupting to emphasize our outrage and we were escorted out. And then nothing happened. (Valot, 2011, para. 14)

The *LA Jewish Journal* reported that 31 faculty at UCR also joined voices at UC campuses statewide in support of the 11 students arrested. Professors and graduate students from several UCR departments signed a "Statement on Free Speech, Palestine and the 'UC Irvine 11,'" drafted by Dylan Rodriguez, chair of the university's ethnic studies department. The March 11 pronouncement called on the UC administration and the Office of the Orange County District Attorney to drop disciplinary and punitive action against the eight UCI and three UCR students, which it called "discriminatory, cynical, and politically and intellectually repressive" (Armony, 2010, para. 1–2). The statement declared:

> We believe that this is a cynical and opportunistic attempt at political repression that reflects the racial criminalization of young Arab, Middle Eastern and Muslim men and women as actual or potential "terrorists." By way of contrast, Ethnic Studies faculty have taught courses in Ethnic Studies in which classroom proceedings were disrupted by students with opposing views, and the university administration did not pursue any disciplinary or punitive measures against them. In fact, we have sometimes been told that such disruptions are an expression of academic free speech. (Armony, 2010, para. 4).

Rodriguez said the statement was intended to take issue with the tendency, since at least 2001, to affiliate Muslim men with terrorism within popular discourse, as well as to challenge what he sees as selective enforcement of codes of conduct by university administrators. "People protesting is something to be expected," he said, noting that UCR administrators did not take disciplinary action against what he called "conservative" student protesters following a similar incident the previous fall. According to Armony (2010), "When people get selectively subjugated to enforcement of codes of conduct, it has a chilling effect on political discussion and freedom (para. 6).

Ten of the students went on trial September 7, 2011, continuing through the 10-year anniversary of 9/11. The defense attorneys argued that a guilty verdict would chill student activism and the free exchange of ideas at colleges nationwide. University administrators disciplined some of the students involved and suspended the campus Muslim Student Union, whose members participated in the protest, for an academic quarter. The group was still on probation at the time of the trial, over a year and a half later (Santa Cruz & Anton, 2011).

After two weeks of trial and two days of jury deliberation, all 10 students were found guilty in Orange County Superior Court of the crimes alleged. Although they were sentenced to no jail time, they were placed on three years of criminal probation and all 10 now have criminal records (Santa Cruz & Anton, 2011).

Similar patterns of systemic repression and exceptional disciplining of students supporting Palestinian solidarity and rights can be seen across the nation (Mac an Ghalil & Haywood, 2017). Muslim students who support Palestinian rights as a human rights issue do so in an atmosphere fraught with fear of negative repercussions to their educational and work opportunities, as well as criminalization of their activism. According to Mac an Ghalil and Haywood (2017),

> Many young Muslim and Arab Americans worry about the real threat of vilification and intimidation if they publicly support Palestine and some distance themselves from a politics defined as 'radical,' which has become a dirty word associated with 'bad' Muslim and Arab subjects. (p. 108)

The Center for Constitutional Rights and four other civil rights organizations wrote to UC president Mark Yudof on December 3, 2012, to express their "collective alarm about developments at University of California (UC) campuses that threaten students' civil rights and forsake the University's responsibility to make the campus welcoming for a range of political viewpoints on the Israeli-Palestinian conflict" (Abunimah, 2012, para. 3). The letter detailed disturbing examples of how the climate of fear of Muslim students instigated by powerful outside groups and lobbies and tolerated by the UC administration had a palpable, chilling effect on students exercising their rights. These included examples of Muslim and Palestinian rights activists on campuses being subject to violent threats and racist language, as well as fraudulent complaints under Title VI of the Civil Rights Act designed to restrict Palestinian rights activism on campuses (Abunimah, 2012).

Clock Boy

On September 14, 2015, Ahmed Mohamed, a 14-year-old Irving, Texas, high school student and avid hobbyist, assembled a clock using a circuit board and digital display and proudly brought the clock to school to show to his teachers. One of his teachers heard the device beeping, thought it resembled a bomb, and brought Mohamed to the principal's office. Local law enforcement was called and Mohamed was questioned by police for an hour and a half. After being handcuffed and taken into custody without being permitted to see his parents, he was arrested and transported to a juvenile detention facility, where he was fingerprinted and his mug shot was taken. It was alleged that the reason for his arrest was for purposely trying to cause a bomb scare (Becket, 2017).

This 14-year-old boy was arrested for making a clock. He was handcuffed, despite the fact that he was a child and posed no threat to law enforcement's safety. After he was handcuffed, questioned at length without permission to see his parents, and arrested without justifiable probable cause, police finally determined Mohamed had no malicious intent. He was ultimately not charged with any crime; however, Mohamed suffered the public humiliation and stress of being arrested and was suspended from school for three days, without valid justification.

The incident ignited allegations of racial profiling and Islamophobia from some media and commentators, and Ahmed Mohamed became known as "Clock Boy." News of the incident became viral—initially on Twitter—with the hashtag #IStandWithAhmed. Even President Obama tweeted, "Cool clock, Ahmed. Want to bring it to the White House? We should inspire more kids like you to like science. It's what makes America great" (quoted in Fantz, Almasy, & Stapleton, 2015, para. 14). Although Mohamed was cleared in the final police investigation, there were unsupported accusations that the incident was a deliberate hoax to bring a fake bomb to school, something that coverage of the incident described as a conspiracy theory. Mohamed's father filed a federal lawsuit in August 2016 against the school district, MacArthur High School's principal, and the city of Irving, Texas, alleging officials violated the boy's civil rights (Becket, 2017, para. 4). In May 2017, the U.S. District Court for the Northern District of Texas incredulously dismissed the claims against the city and the school district, writing that the court could not "reasonably infer that any employee intentionally discriminated against [Mohamed] based on his race or religion" (para. 6).

The Ongoing Surveillance of Muslim Students

The aftermath of the Associated Press's widely acclaimed reporting in 2011 and subsequent outcry prompted the closure of the Demographics Unit by New York City mayor Bill de Blasio and created the impression of a new era of policing. Many wrongly assumed that suspicionless surveillance of Muslims was no longer occurring. Two lawsuits filed against the NYPD by Muslims who had been subjected to surveillance settled, appearing to seal the deal, and news outlets covering the settlement used the past tense to describe NYPD's surveillance of Muslims (Apuzzo & Goldstein, 2014).

The short documentary *Watched* (Mitchell, 2017), which first premiered at the Tribeca Film Festival in April 2017, reveals, however, that this is far from the case. *Watched* tells the story of two Muslim students preyed upon by a female undercover NYPD officer, "Mel," who came to Brooklyn College (BC) to spy on Muslim and political students from 2011 to 2015. Mel spent the majority of her time at BC after the publication of the groundbreaking Associated Press reports, and her presence continued for more than a year after de Blasio came into office. *Watched* serves as an undeniable rebuttal to the notion that mass surveillance of Muslim New Yorkers is a thing of the past (Stahl & Theoharis, 2017).

Mel's persona at BC was that she was interested in exploring her religious roots because she was raised in a secular Turkish family. On her first day on campus she converted to Islam with a group of Muslim students as her witnesses. She attended events and participated in discussions regarding Muslim students' religious and political believes for four years. She was welcomed with open arms to Muslim students' homes, to picnics, and other gatherings. She also served as bridesmaid in a wedding. The NYPD admitted that an undercover operative was sent to BC in an "approved investigation," but nothing came of this investigation (Stahl & Theoharis, 2017).

In "The Ongoing Trauma of the Muslim Students an Undercover Cop Spied on for 4 Years," Aviva Stahl and Jeanne Theoharis (2017) poignantly write about the impact of *Watched*, stating,

> The film charts the devastating effects of such prolonged surveillance: the anxiety and self-doubt it produced in students, the diminishing of what these political and religious young women felt they could do or say, the mistrust it generated amongst students, the way it made them feel less safe in public, and the fears of being jailed like other Muslims they knew. Fundamentally, even as the election of Donald Trump has brought the issue of Islamophobia to the fore, *Watched* is a rare portrayal of the devastating impacts of policing on young Muslim lives. While Muslim Americans are constantly talked about in the public sphere, we seldom hear their unmediated voices. *Watched* is a rare journalistic endeavor, one in which we are able to listen to American Muslim women speak about their experiences coming of age in post-9/11 America—without any other voices cutting in. (para. 3)

In an October 2017 op-ed article titled "'Random' Searches Criminalize Students and Don't Make Schools Safer," John Marshall High School student Grace Hamilton writes that "dozens of times a day, school deans and security walk into Los Angeles Unified School District classrooms and pick out five students to conduct a 'random' search" (Hamilton, 2017, para. 1). She details that students are taken "out of class and into the hallway, where these school officials go through [their] belongings. [Students] are told they are searching them for weapons, but they frequently take classroom supplies, like white-out and highlighters" (para. 1). Although the searches are supposed to be random, they are not. Hamilton notes that Muslim students are one of the groups "targeted for searches based on stereotypes that make them out to be dangerous" (para. 4). Hamilton also states, "The only purpose these 'random' searches serve is to criminalize, traumatize, and degrade racial and ethnic groups in schools" (para. 5).

Negative Impact of Targeting Muslims

In this post-9/11 era, Muslim students nationwide have experienced disparate treatment by school safety officers, school and law enforcement officials, and teachers alike. Through religious profiling and surveillance, an unwarranted badge of suspicion and stigma has been thrust on law-abiding Muslim students. The criminalization and unlawful profiling of Muslims has damaged law enforcement relationships with American Muslims, violating the communities' trust in any law enforcement officer who is tasked with protecting and serving them.

This discriminatory surveillance and treatment has produced an undeniable atmosphere of fear and mistrust on school campuses nationwide, chilling religious speech and political activism and discouraging Muslim students from participating in robust, healthy forms of debate and protest. Moreover, by criminalizing behavior of Muslim students that need not, and should not, be treated as such, we are encouraging and perpetuating the institutionalization of Islamophobia within our schools and across the nation at large. The following section offers recommendations that will help curb surveillance and criminalization of Muslim students, deinstitutionalize Islamophobia, and combat discrimination.

Recommendations

This chapter focused on how law enforcement such as the FBI, CIA, and police agencies have used various methods to spy on and monitor Muslim communities without any suspicion of wrongdoing. Through a discussion of cases like Mostafa Tabatabainejad, the Irvine 11, and Clock Boy, this chapter illustrated how Muslims have been criminalized, how they continue to be surveilled, and how such acts have a negative impact on the Muslim community at large and Muslim students specifically. As such, it is recommended that institutions of higher education add classes discussing Islamic religion, cultures, and politics, while noting significant and contributing Muslims in the United States, into university curriculum in order to inform students and create an atmosphere of awareness. Such changes in the curriculum will aid in eradicating inherent bias and fear-based responses. Additionally, inviting prominent Muslims in the community and society at large to speak at university campuses will introduce students and faculty to actual prominent and contributing members of society—real Muslims who are making a positive impact in the United States and the world at large. Finally, encouraging the formation and growth of Muslim Student Associations on campuses will hopefull recruit a diverse array of individuals who will work together to promote community and awareness.

Discussion Questions

1. Can you cite examples of ignorance of culture or religion in U.S. history that have contributed to fear-based action in the past?
2. How has increasing awareness and familiarity within your own lives made you more comfortable interacting and accepting those who are different from you?
3. What changes can your institution make to facilitate dialogue between Muslim and non-Muslim students and encourage an atmosphere of awareness and community?
4. How can law enforcement and university police be trained to ensure Muslim students are treated fairly and in an unbiased manner?

References

Abunimah, A. (2012, December 4). *Climate of fear silencing Palestinian, Muslim students at University of California, rights groups warn.* Retrieved from https://electronicintifada.net/blogs/ali-abunimah/climate-fear-silencing-palestinian-muslim-students-university-california-rights

ACLU. (2017, June 17). *Factsheet: The NYPD Muslim surveillance program.* Retrieved from https://www.aclu.org/other/factsheet-nypd-muslim-surveillance-program

Apuzzo, A., & Goldstein, J. (2014, April 15). New York drops unit that spied on Muslims. *New York Times.* Retrieved from https://www.nytimes.com/2014/04/16/nyregion/police-unit-that-spied-on-muslims-is-disbanded.html

Armony, L. (2010, March 16). UC Riverside faculty voice support for protesters against Oren. *Jewish Journal.* Retrieved from https://jewishjournal.com/news/los_angeles/community/77569/

Associated Press. (2012, April 16). AP wins Pulitzer Prize for Investigative Reporting on NYPD surveillance [Press release]. Retrieved from https://www.ap.org/press-releases/2012/ap-wins-pulitzer-prize-for-investigative-reporting-on-nypd-surveillance

Becket, S. (2017, May 19). "Clock Boy" discrimination lawsuit dismissed by federal judge. *CBS News.* Retrieved from https://www.cbsnews.com/news/clock-boy-ahmed-mohamed-discrimination-lawsuit-dismissed/

Bobb, M., Barge, M., & Naguib, C. (2007, August). *A bad night at Powell Library: The events of November 14, 2006.* Retrieved from https://static1.squarespace.com/static/5498b74ce4b01fe317ef2575/t/54ae9f26e4b0118189026 97d/1420730150743/UCLA+Taser+Report+August+Final.pdf

Centers for Disease Control and Prevention. (2002, September 9). *Deaths in World Trade Center terrorist attacks—New York City, 2001.* Retrieved from https://www.cdc.gov/mmwr/preview/mmwrhtml/mm51spa6.htm

Council on American-Islamic Relations. (2013, December 19). *Growing in faith: California Muslim youth experiences with bullying, harassment and religious accommodation in schools.* Washington, DC: Author.

Disturbing a Public Meeting, Cal. Penal Code §403 (1872 & rev. 1994). Retrieved from https://leginfo.legislature.ca.gov/faces/codes_displaySection.xhtml?lawCode=PEN&sectionNum=403.#

Fantz, A., Almasy, S., & Stapleton, A. (2015, September 16). Muslim teen Ahmed Mohamed creates clock, shows teachers, gets arrested. *CNN.* Retrieved from https://www.cnn.com/2015/09/16/us/texas-student-ahmed-muslim-clock-bomb/index.html

Fishkoff, S. (2011, March 9). Drop charges against "Irvine 11." *Jewish Telegraphic Agency.* Retrieved from https://www.jta.org/2011/03/09/united-states/drop-charges-against-irvine-11-jewish-faculty-urges

Goldman, A., & Apuzzo, M. (2012, August 21). NYPD: Muslim spying led to no leads, terror cases. *AP.* Retrieved from https://www.ap.org/ap-in-the-news/2012/nypd-muslim-spying-led-to-no-leads-terror-cases

Greenwald, G. (2013, March 19). The FBI's anticipatory prosecution of Muslims to criminalize speech. *Guardian.* Retrieved from https://www.theguardian.com/commentisfree/2013/mar/19/preemptive-prosecution-muslims-cointelpro

Hamilton, G. (2017, October 20). "Random" searches criminalize students and don't make schools safer. *UTLA.* Retrieved from https://www.utla.net/news/random-searches-criminalize-students-and-dont-make-schools-safer

Harris, B. (2010, February 19). Jewish leaders want U.C. Irvine to react powerfully. *J.* Retrieved from https://www.jweekly.com/2010/02/19/jewish-leaders-want-u-c-irvine-to-react-powerfully/

Jolly, V., Galvin, A., & Hernandez, S. (2011, February 5). *11 Muslim students face charges in UCI protest.* Retrieved from https://www.ocregister.com/2011/02/05/11-muslim-students-face-charges-in-uci-protest/

Mac an Ghalil, M., & Haywood, C. (2017). *Muslim students, education, and neoliberalism: Schooling a suspect community*. London, UK: Palgrave Macmillan.

Medina, J. (2011, February 9). Charges against Muslim students prompt debate over free speech. *New York Times*. Retrieved from https://www.nytimes.com/2011/02/10/education/10irvine.html

Mitchell, K. (Director). (2017). *Watched* [Film]. D. Menschel (Executive Producder), K. Mitchell, and D. Varga (Producers).

Santa Cruz, N., & Anton, M. (2011, September 23). "Irvine 11" jury finds all 10 students guilty. *LA Times*. Retrieved from https://latimesblogs.latimes.com/lanow/2011/09/irvine-11-verdict-1.html

Sikh Coalition. (2014). *"Go home, Terrorist": A report on bullying against Sikh American school children*. New York, NY: Author.

Stahl, A., & Theoharis, J. (2017, April 21). The ongoing trauma of the Muslim students an undercover cop spied on for 4 years. *Vice*. Retrieved from https://broadly.vice.com/en_us/article/bjgz4z/the-ongoing-trauma-of-the-muslim-students-an-undercover-cop-spied-on-for-4-years

Turbanhead. (2006, November 15). UCLA student gets tasered [Video file]. *YouTube*. Retrieved from https://www.youtube.com/watch?v=4JGlvEcPmug

UCLA taser incident. (n.d.). *Wikipedia*. Retrieved from https://en.wikipedia.org/wiki/UCLA_Taser_incident

Valot, S. (2011, February 9). Jewish community shows support for Muslim student protestors. *KPCC News*. Retrieved from https://www.scpr.org/news/2011/02/09/23891/jewish-community-shows-support-muslim-student-prot/

3

THE MUSLIM BANS, HUMAN RIGHTS, AND INTERNATIONAL MUSLIM STUDENTS

Zulaikha Aziz

On January 27, 2017, President Trump attempted to fulfill his campaign pledge "calling for a total and complete shutdown of Muslims entering the United States" (Johnson, 2015, para. 7) by signing Executive Order 13,769 banning nationals from seven Muslim-majority countries from traveling to and entering the United States. That Friday marked the beginning of a chaotic and fearful period for many Muslims in the United States and around the world—a period marked by separation of families and loved ones; loss of employment or educational opportunities; and, in some cases, return to conflict and war. Though this original travel ban was met with swift and sharp challenges, both in the courts and on the streets, President Trump issued a second equally flawed ban to replace it, this time with Presidential Proclamation 9,645.

In addition to the myriad practical impacts of the consecutive travel bans, they also serve as a reminder to Muslims that they are not wanted in the United States by the current president and his administration. Muslims' right to practice their faith is pitted against their right to be free of discrimination, to be subject to the same laws regulating asylum and immigration to the United States as every other religious group. This blatant form of discrimination is illegal under not only U.S. domestic law but also international law, namely international human rights treaties we as a country have signed, ratified, and in many cases drafted over the past 60 years.

Though the impacts of the Muslim travel ban are wide and profound, this chapter will focus on the implications of the ban to U.S. human rights obligations under international law and the impact of the ban on international students attending or seeking to attend universities in the United States. This chapter will also touch on the harmful effects of the ban on academia in the United States more generally and offer recommendations on how academic institutions may support students and also comply with international human rights standards while navigating the travel ban.

History of the Muslim Travel Ban

The first so-called Muslim ban, or Executive Order 13,769, was signed on January 27, 2017. It was quickly halted by a number of lawsuits filed across the country. In the few days it was enforced, it created mass havoc and confusion among Muslim travelers from impacted countries and beyond. The impact of the Muslim travel ban was clearly tied to the president's intent in enacting the ban. In attempting to accomplish his campaign promise of banning Muslims from the United States, he started with the countries of Iran, Iraq, Libya, Somalia, Sudan, Syria, and Yemen. Executive Order 13,769 barred the resettlement of Syrian refugees indefinitely and blocked the entry of citizens from all seven predominantly Muslim countries for a period of 120 days. The order slashed and suspended refugee resettlement, directing that future priority be given to "refugee claims made by individuals on the basis of religious-based persecution, provided that the religion of the individual is a minority religion in the individual's country of nationality" (Executive Order No. 13,769, 2017a, para. 17)—a blatant restriction on the resettlement of Muslim refugees from Muslim-majority countries. The order also included a specific exception for religious minorities (i.e., non-Muslims) from the listed Muslim countries.

Executive Order 13,769 violated the U.S. obligation to refugee resettlement by completely prohibiting resettlement of refugees for 120 days and indefinitely banning refugees from Syria. The order stated it would lower the number of refugees to be admitted into the United States in 2017 to 50,000, down from 85,000 in 2016; "suspend the U.S. Refugee Admissions Program (USRAP) for 120 days"; and "suspend the entry of Syrian refugees indefinitely" (Executive Order No. 13,769, 2017a, para. 16). Its requirement of suspension of entry of immigrants from certain countries, *even with valid visas or travel documents* (Executive Order No. 13,769, 2017a) was in violation of U.S. immigration law.

The order resulted in massive chaos and confusion at airports around the world. Thousands of travelers were thrown into uncertainty as families were separated at ports of disembarkation, approved refugees were denied boarding, lawful permanent residents were detained at airports for hours on end, and valid visa holders were refused entry and even deported. Department of Homeland Security border control officials had not been given adequate instructions and were at a loss in applying the muddled order. As the order was legally binding on them and yet was in direct contradiction of U.S. immigration laws, there was expected pandemonium at the airports.

Many Muslim students studying at U.S. academic institutions were caught in the mess. A PhD student at Stanford University and lawful permanent resident of the United States originally from Sudan "had been in Sudan for academic research and boarded a plane on Friday morning. After presenting her U.S. green card, a designation of legal permanent residence, at JFK, she said she was questioned, patted down and handcuffed" (Dobunzinskis, 2017, para. 4).

The American public showed up en masse to airports around the country to lend support and comfort to those affected. In response to a deluge of lawsuits brought by a number of states and private parties, on February 3, 2017, a nationwide temporary restraining order was issued in the case *State of Washington and State of Minnesota v. Trump* (2017), which was upheld by the U.S. Court of Appeals for the Ninth Circuit. The Department of Homeland Security was forced to stop enforcing portions of the order and the State Department was required to revalidate visas that had been previously revoked.

The Trump administration issued Executive Order 13,780 on March 6, 2017, in an attempt to ameliorate some of the more egregious portions of the original order after its invalidation (Executive Order No. 13,780, 2017b). The new order made explicit the exclusion of permanent residents and those with valid current visas from the ban. The new order also excluded Iraq from the list of banned countries after Iraq threatened to expel all U.S. citizen contractors from its borders.

In response to Executive Order 13,780, new lawsuits were filed, and on March 15, 2017, the U.S. District Court for the District of Hawaii, citing comments made by Trump and his administration, found that the executive order was likely motivated by anti-Muslim sentiment and thus breached the Establishment Clause of the United States Constitution (*State of Hawaii v. Trump*, 2017). The court issued a temporary restraining order, as did a number of other federal district courts (State of *Hawaii v. Trump*, 2017). The Trump administration appealed to the U.S. Supreme Court, which partially lifted the temporary restraining order and stayed the lower court injunctions as applied to those who have no "credible claim of a bona fide relationship with a person or entity in the United States" and agreed to hear oral arguments, which were scheduled for October 10, 2017 (*Trump v. International Refugee Assistance Project*, 2017, p. 12). In its unsigned ruling, the court specifically stated that students from the designated countries who have been admitted to a university are considered to have a "bona fide relationship" (p. 12) with an American entity. This was also the case for workers who accepted offers of employment from an American company (i.e., for those on J-1 Research Scholar status, Post-Completion OPT, or who are pending a change of status to H-1B). Since then, the administration has defined *bona fide relationship* as including certain familial relationships and not others and has rejected the relationship between refugees and official resettlement organizations.

On September 24, 2017, President Trump issued Presidential Proclamation 9,645, which imposed new travel restrictions on the entry of foreign nationals from an expanded eight countries: Chad, Iran, Libya, North Korea, Somalia, Syria, Venezuela, and Yemen (Proclamation No. 9,645, 2017). North Korea and Venezuela were added to the travel restrictions list, and Sudan was removed. Chad was later removed on April 11, 2018 ("Trump Lifts Travel Ban on Chad," 2018). In response, the Supreme Court canceled its hearing and granted the government's request to declare the Maryland case moot and vacate that judgment because the government had in effect nullified Executive Order 13,780. The Supreme Court allowed the new ban to go into full effect, pending new legal challenges.

This third iteration of the travel ban sets travel restrictions on each of the eight countries, claiming that the secretary of Homeland Security assessed the eight countries to "have 'inadequate' identity-management protocols, information-sharing practices, and risk factors . . . such that entry restrictions and limitations are recommended" (Proclamation No. 9,645, 2017, para. 10). Proclamation 9,645 suspends all immigrant and nonimmigrant visas for nationals of Syria and North Korea. All immigrant and nonimmigrant visas are likewise suspended for nationals from Iran, except for F (student), M (vocational student), and J (exchange visitor) visas, which will be subject to "enhanced screening and vetting requirements" (para. 18). Immigrant visas and nonimmigrant business (B-1) and tourist (B-2) visas are suspended for nationals of Libya and Yemen. The proclamation suspends all immigrant visas and requires "additional scrutiny" (para. 12) of all nonimmigrant visas issued for Somali nationals. Last, the proclamation suspends business and tourist visas for certain Venezuelan government officials and their immediate family members. The proclamation excludes lawful permanent residents of the United States, dual-nationals traveling on passports from nondesignated countries, asylees, and refugees already admitted to the United States, but does not provide any exclusion for others, including refugees who have applied for asylum but not been approved yet.

Unlike the two prior travel bans, the third ban has no end date. It only allows for the granting of waivers on a case-by-case basis if an individual "has previously been admitted to the United States for a continuous period of work, study, or other long-term activity," "has previously established significant contacts with the United States," "seeks to enter the United States to visit or reside with a close family member (e.g., a spouse, child, or parent) who is a United States citizen," or "has been employed by, or on behalf of, the United States Government" (Proclamation No. 9,645, 2017, para. 26). Although Proclamation 9,645 is couched in national security language, it is a clear attempt to make good on Trump's discriminatory campaign pledge to impose a "total and complete shutdown of Muslims entering the United States" (Johnson, 2015, para. 7).

Of note, though Proclamation 9,645 includes Venezuela and North Korea, the impact on those countries' nationals is very narrow, because the Venezuelan designation is limited to business and tourist visas for certain government officials and their family members and, though all North Korean nationals are included, reportedly only 109 North Koreans received visas in 2016 out of more than 75 million visitors to the United States ("US Expands Travel Ban to Include North Korea," 2017). This third version of the travel ban remains a ban on Muslims. Venezuela as a country is not banned; only certain government officials and their families are affected, and those individuals are barred only from obtaining tourist and temporary business visas. As for North Korea, the number of nationals seeking to travel to the United States is negligible. In contrast, nearly every single person from the Muslim-majority countries is barred from getting a green card, no matter what family, business, or other U.S. connections they have.

This latest version of the Muslim travel ban encountered the same legal obstacles as its two predecessors. In a 9–4 vote, on February 15, 2018, the Fourth U.S. Circuit Court of Appeals in Richmond, Virginia, concluded that Proclamation 9,645 is unconstitutionally tainted with animus toward Islam (*International Refugee Assistance Project v. Trump*, 2017a). The court upheld a ruling by a federal judge in Maryland who issued an injunction barring enforcement of the ban against people from Chad, Iran, Libya, Somalia, Syria, and Yemen who have bona fide relationships with people in the United States. In its ruling, the Fourth Circuit used soaring language to criticize the ban, saying it had a "much broader deleterious effect" (*International Refugee Assistance Project v. Trump*, 2017b, p. 56) than banning certain foreign nationals. The court said the ban "denies the possibility of a complete, intact family to tens of thousands of Americans" (p. 57). Chief Justice Roger Gregory wrote that "on a fundamental level, the proclamation second-guesses our nation's dedication to religious freedom and tolerance" (p. 57). The ruling was the second time the Fourth Circuit has rejected a travel ban. In

May, the court cited Trump's remarks on Muslim travelers while rejecting an earlier version of the ban, finding it "drips with religious intolerance, animus and discrimination" (*International Refugee Assistance Project v. Trump*, 2017a, p. 12). It had been found to be discriminatory by all courts hearing the case but was ultimately found to be valid by the U.S. Supreme Court in a very controversial 5–4 decision.

But this third version of the ban has been upheld by the U.S. Supreme Court as the law of our land. On June 26, 2018, the court issued a controversial 5–4 decision in *Trump v. Hawaii* (2018), upholding Muslim Ban 3.0. In a troubling endorsement of executive overreach, the majority found that the proclamation did not exceed the president's statutory power (*Trump v. Hawaii*, 2018). However, in her dissenting opinion, Justice Sotomayor, joined by Justice Ginsburg, found that the Muslim ban was clearly motivated by unconstitutional animus. Justice Sotomayor states that "the full record paints a far more harrowing picture, from which a reasonable observer would readily conclude that the Proclamation was motivated by hostility and animus toward the Muslim faith" (*Trump v. Hawaii*, 2018, p. 4). She draws parallels to the U.S. Supreme Court's 1944 *Korematsu v. United States* decision, which upheld the legality of Executive Order 9,066 (1942) and the incarceration of over 120,000 Japanese Americans in internment camps during World War II:

> By blindly accepting the government's misguided invitation to sanction a discriminatory policy motivated by animosity toward a disfavored group, all in the name of a superficial claim of national security, the court redeploys the same dangerous logic underlying *Korematsu* and merely replaces one "gravely wrong" decision with another. (*Trump v. Hawaii*, 2018, para. 28)

Finally, in his dissenting opinion, Justice Breyer, joined by Justice Kagan, flagged concerns with the waiver process, and added that by excluding individuals who are not detrimental to the United States, the U.S. government's national security justifications for the sweeping order are significantly weakened.

International Human Rights Treaties and the United States

A fundamental purpose for the existence of international laws, and the international human rights framework in particular, is to provide an overarching layer of protection against abuses of a set of rights so fundamental to our humanity that the community of nations has agreed they are to be universally secured. The international human rights framework was developed in large part in response to the actions of countries during the World War I and

World War II, which constituted such grave violations that it was decided those actions should never be possible again. Many of those violations were committed in the name of national security. Since then, international law has learned from past errors and made explicit that no such violations can be excused by an appeal to national security, nor be permitted by an appeal to xenophobia (Dakwar, 2017).

Human rights are activities, conditions, and freedoms that all human beings are entitled to enjoy, by virtue of their humanity. Human rights are inherent, inalienable, interdependent, and indivisible. They cannot be granted or taken away, the enjoyment of one right affects the enjoyment of others, and they must all be respected. International human rights norms have developed over time and are long-standing shared universal beliefs regarding rights that all humans have. International human rights are based on *jus cogens*—certain fundamental, overriding principles of international law that are deemed to be so fundamental to our collective humanity that they are held to be universally accepted and from which no derogation is permitted regardless of whether they are codified.

Human rights can be enforced both domestically and internationally. Domestically, national governments have power to put in place national laws and policies necessary for protection of human rights and to regulate private and public practices that impact individuals' enjoyment of those rights. In the international sphere, nations have come up with a system of legally binding agreements or covenants to which they agree to be bound in the furtherance of a set of international laws they have universally agreed are important to uphold. International human rights treaties are covenants between those nations and the international community, whereby nations agree to guarantee certain rights within their own territories.

The United Nations Charter, signed in 1945, acknowledged the importance of human rights and established it as a matter of international concern. Article 1(3) specifically states that one of the purposes of the United Nations is "promoting and encouraging respect for human rights and for fundamental freedoms for all without distinction as to race, sex, language, or religion" (UN Charter art. 1, para. 3). Articles 55 and 56 of the charter set out the basic human rights obligations of the UN and its member states (UN Charter art. 55–56). The rights and obligations enumerated in the charter were codified in the Universal Declaration of Human Rights, the first modern instrument to articulate the fundamental rights and freedoms of all people. Following the Universal Declaration, the UN Commission on Human Rights drafted the International Covenant on Civil and Political Rights and the International Covenant on Economic, Social and Cultural Rights. These three documents together comprise the International Bill of Human Rights.

In the United States, ratified international treaties are considered legally binding as "the highest law of the land" under the Supremacy Clause of the U.S. Constitution, which gives acceded treaties the status of federal law (U.S. Const. art. VI, cl. 2). As a matter of domestic law, an international agreement is regarded as a treaty if it has received the "advice and consent" of two-thirds of the Senate and has been ratified by the president (U.S. Const. art. II, § 2, cl. 2). Ratified treaties are legally binding internationally but can be enforced in domestic courts only if they are self-executing or if they have been enacted by Congress. If an international treaty is not self-executing, it becomes binding in domestic courts when implemented by an official act of Congress. The United States has both ratified self-executing international treaties prohibiting discrimination against refugees and immigrants *and* enacted domestic legislation to the same effect.

International Human Rights Treaties Violated by the Muslim Ban

Although national governments are responsible for designing their own refugee resettlement and immigration schemes, they must conform to existing international obligations. The United States is subject to all treaties and international agreements it has entered into and ratified, if self-executing, or enacted as part of its domestic laws if the treaty is not self-executing. The United States is legally obligated, in both the international sphere and the domestic sphere, to select refugees for resettlement only on the basis of their needs, regardless of nationality, ethnicity, religion, or other related characteristics. Similarly, the United States is obligated to apply its domestic immigration laws in a nondiscriminatory manner in line with domestic nondiscrimination prohibitions and international human rights laws.

Universal Declaration of Human Rights

The Universal Declaration of Human Rights (UDHR) is a declaratory document that sets up the international human rights framework and all of the conventions that arise from it; it is the cornerstone from which all modern international human rights law arises (UN General Assembly, 1948). It also sets out the basic fundamentals and guiding principles of human rights law, including the principle of nondiscrimination in the application of human rights. The UDHR, which was adopted by the UN General Assembly on December 10, 1948, was the result of the experience of the Second World War. With the end of that war and the creation of the United Nations, the international community vowed never to allow the atrocities experienced during that war to occur again. The United States is not only a party to the

UDHR but also a lead drafter and a prominent advocate for the adoption of an international human rights framework under Franklin D. Roosevelt's presidency (UN UDHR, 2015).

Article 2 of the UDHR states, "Everyone is entitled to all the rights and freedoms set forth in this Declaration, without distinction of any kind, such as race, colour, sex, language, religion, political or other opinion, national or social origin, property, birth or other status" (UN General Assembly, 1948). Article 7 affirms that "all are equal before the law and are entitled without any discrimination to equal protection of the law" (UN General Assembly, 1948). All are entitled to equal protection against any discrimination in violation of the UDHR and against any incitement to such discrimination. In regard to refugee protections, Article 14 of the UDHR specifically recognizes the right of persons to seek asylum from persecution in other countries (UN General Assembly, 1948).

Though the UDHR is not a legally binding document, it sets out the underlying principles of the human rights framework, which are enshrined in subsequent legally binding documents. The travel ban, in intent, language, and application, is in direct contravention of the UDHR. By specifically targeting Muslim refugees and immigrants, U.S. courts have found that the travel ban "drips with religious intolerance, animus and discrimination" (*International Refugee Assistance Project v. Trump*, 2017). This is in direct violation of UDHR Articles 2 and 7, requiring state-parties to provide all persons the rights to which they are entitled without distinction to religion or national or social origin and apply all domestic laws equally, providing equal protection of the laws. By specifically targeting refugees, and entirely excluding refugees from Syria, the travel ban is also in violation of Article 14 of the UDHR, enjoining state-parties to recognize the right of all persons to seek asylum from persecution in other countries.

1951 Convention Relating to the Status of Refugees and Its 1967 Protocol

The 1951 Convention Relating to the Status of Refugees and its 1967 Protocol (Refugee Convention) follows from Article 14 of the UDHR (UN General Assembly, 1951). The Refugee Convention is the foundation of international refugee law today. The United States did not join the Refugee Convention in 1951 because the convention's initial application was limited to the context of refugees in Europe resulting from World War I and World War II. The United States became a party to the 1967 Protocol, ratified in 1968, when it amended the Refugee Convention by removing the geographic and temporal limits of the initial version and giving it universal application (UN High Commissioner for Refugees [UNHCR], 2011). As a member of the Refugee Convention, the United States is obligated to comply with its objective and purpose, which include duties to accept applications for asylum of persons found in its territory and not return persons to states where they will face persecution or torture.

The Refugee Convention requires that the United States provide protection and safe haven to those fleeing persecution regardless of race, religion, or nationality. By barring Muslim refugees fleeing severe conditions of war and persecution, Proclamation 9,645 blatantly violates this core U.S. obligation to refugees. Article 3 of the Refugee Convention makes clear that all signatory states, including the United States, must "apply the provisions . . . to refugees without discrimination as to race, religion or country of origin" (UN General Assembly, 1951). The ban on refugees from Syria is in direct violation of Article 3, as it targets a vulnerable population based solely on religion and national origin.

International Convention on the Elimination of All Forms of Racial Discrimination

The International Convention on the Elimination of All Forms of Racial Discrimination (ICERD) lays out specific standards and steps countries that are state-parties should take to prevent, eliminate, and redress racism and racial discrimination (UN General Assembly, 1965). ICERD was signed by the United States in 1966 and ratified in 1994, making it legally binding on all levels of government. Though the United States has a relatively strong civil rights tradition of nondiscrimination, ICERD goes beyond the requirements of U.S. domestic law in a number of key ways. ICERD requires state-parties to "guarantee the right of everyone, without distinction as to race, colour, or national or ethnic origin, to equality before the law" (UN General Assembly, 1965). ICERD explicitly prohibits discrimination based on nationality in regard to immigration policy under Article 1(3), and Article 2(c) notes that the discrimination may include "any laws . . . which have the effect of creating or perpetuating racial discrimination" (UN General Assembly, 1965).

In 2008, the Committee on the Elimination of Racial Discrimination (CERD), the committee set up to monitor ICERD, specifically addressed the U.S. government's racial profiling of Arabs, Muslims, and South Asians after the 9/11 attacks and the development of the National Security Entry-Exit Registration System for nationals of 25 countries, all located in the Middle East, South Asia, or North Africa. CERD warned that "measures taken in the struggle against terrorism must not discriminate, in purpose or effect, on the grounds of race, colour, descent, or national or ethnic origin" (UN

CERD, 2004). Analogously, Proclamation 9,645 specifically targets persons from six nationalities, in direct violation of ICERD.

International Covenant on Civil and Political Rights

The International Covenant on Civil and Political Rights (ICCPR) establishes universal standards for the protection of basic civil and political liberties (UN General Assembly, 1966). Though the United States took part in the drafting of ICCPR, the United States delayed signing the covenant until 1977 and ratifying it until 1992. ICCPR commits state-parties to respect the civil and political rights of individuals, including the right to life, freedom of religion, freedom of speech, freedom of assembly, electoral rights, and rights to due process and a fair trial. Several of its articles specifically prohibit discrimination under the color of law.

Article 2 of ICCPR forbids state-parties from making distinctions in the provision of civil and political rights based on "race, colour, sex, language, religion, political or other opinion, national or social origin, property, birth or other status" (UN General Assembly, 1966). Article 26 requires equal treatment before the law of all persons, without discrimination on any ground: "The law shall prohibit any discrimination and guarantee to all persons equal and effective protection against discrimination on any ground such as race, colour, sex, language, religion, political or other opinion, national or social origin, property, birth or other status" (UN General Assembly, 1966). By giving fewer rights to Muslims in their ability to travel to the United States, and in wholly restricting the consideration of a set of Muslim refugees, the United States is in clear violation of Articles 2 and 26 of ICCPR. Article 4 of ICCPR makes clear that even in a "time of public emergency which threatens the life of the nation," states cannot take any action to stray from their obligations that involve discrimination "solely on the ground of race, colour, sex, language, religion or social origin" (UN General Assembly, 1966). The United States cannot justify its violations of ICCPR by invoking national security.

International Convention Against Torture and Other Cruel, Inhuman, or Degrading Treatment or Punishment

Proclamation 9645, by its blanket restriction of all persons from the listed states regardless of their refugee status or risk of torture, also violates a U.S. obligations under the International Convention Against Torture and Other Cruel, Inhuman or Degrading Treatment or Punishment (CAT) (UN General Assembly, 1984). CAT aims to prevent torture and other acts of cruel, inhuman, or degrading treatment or punishment around the world by requiring states to take real measures domestically to prevent torture in any territory under their jurisdiction. CAT was adopted by the United Nations in 1984. The United States signed CAT in 1988 and ratified it in 1992, making it legally binding.

U.S. Obligation of Nonrefoulement

Article 3 of CAT references the principle of nonrefoulement and in effect codifies it as a separate binding duty under the convention. Article 3 forbids state-parties from expelling, returning, or extraditing a person to a state "where there are substantial grounds for believing that he would be in danger of being subjected to torture" (UN General Assembly, 1984, p. 114). By definition, *refugees* flee repressive regimes to escape persecution. Sending people back to a country where they may well suffer torture violates CAT. As a state-party of CAT, the United States has a legally binding duty to not return a noncitizen to a country where they face torture or persecution. By sanctioning the deportation of refugees, the current travel ban is in violation of Article 3 of CAT. The obligation of nonrefoulement is binding on all states regardless of whether they are parties to the Refugee Convention and the Convention Against Torture or not (UNHCR, 2007). This principle is widely understood to be an "essential . . . component of international refugee protection" (UNHCR, 2007, para. 12).

U.S. Domestic Obligations of Nondiscrimination Toward Refugees and Immigrants

In addition to U.S. international obligations of nondiscrimination toward refugees and immigrants, our country has historically been recognized and celebrated for a long-standing tradition of accepting refugees and immigrants. The UNHCR and International Organization for Migration referenced this historic value in recognizing that the "U.S. resettlement program is one of the most important in the world" and the "long-standing U.S. policy of welcoming refugees has . . . saved the lives of some of the most vulnerable people in the world who have in turn enriched and strengthened their new societies," in a joint statement released after the first ban (UNHCR, 2017, para. 1). As further evidence of the long-standing U.S. commitment to refugees, under President Reagan, Congress enacted the Refugee Act (1980) with widespread bipartisan support and established the legal framework for providing refugees access to protection in the United States through the asylum and refugee resettlement systems to bring U.S. refugee law into conformance with the Refugee Convention.

Implications of the Travel Ban on Higher Education in the United States

Given that the current Muslim travel ban is in violation of U.S. international human rights obligations, how are international students and academic institutions in the United States impacted, and what are some steps academic institutions can take to provide guidance and support to counteract the negative impacts of the current ban?

At the most fundamental level, international students from the banned countries are being directly targeted and face direct consequences. They are advised not to return home or travel outside of the United States if they have been accepted or are attending U.S. academic institutions; they are potentially restricted from studying in the United States if they have not yet obtained acceptance. These students not only face direct infringement of their rights to be free of discrimination under U.S. immigration laws but also are subject to reduced opportunities to study and learn in the United States, decreased career opportunities, and severe restrictions on travel and immigration. Muslim students who are already in the United States, whether they are immigrants or not, are also facing negative impacts as a result of the anti-Muslim rhetoric surrounding the bans, including increased incidents of discrimination on and off campus; travel difficulties and restrictions impacting studies, work, and research; and a general fear and anxiety that they are not the same as other students. Consequently, U.S. academia as a whole is impacted by lower admissions of international students, lack of diversity of the student body, less variety of thought and research, and decreased opportunities for cross-cultural communication and collaboration.

Impacts on International Students

Though there had been a 2.4% increase in enrollment of international students during the 2015–2016 academic year, the number of new international students enrolling in U.S. universities fell by 6.6% in the fall of 2017 and the declining trend seems to be holding for the current year (Redden, 2018a). It is not clear whether the decline is due to the hostile climate Trump has created for international students in general and Muslim students in particular; however, an *Inside Higher Ed* analysis of State Department data showed a sharp drop in the number of student visas awarded to students from a number of the countries targeted by the ban (Redden, 2018b). Similarly, though the Institute of International Education's (IIE's) *Open Doors Report* shows a 1.2% increase in the number of Iranian students at the graduate level for fall of 2017, the number of Iranian students did decline by 16.8% at the undergraduate and 35.7% at nondegree levels (IIE, 2018). It should be noted, however, that approximately 75% of Iranian students are at the graduate level (IIE, 2018). Among other countries covered by the various versions of Trump's travel ban, which were in effect for parts of the 2017–2018 application cycle, there was a 15.3% drop in the total number of students from Iraq, an 18.8% drop in students from Libya, a 12.2% decrease in students from Syria, and a 21.4% decrease in students from Yemen (IIE, 2018). At the same time, there were increases in the number of students from Somalia (34%) and Sudan (2.2%) (IIE, 2018).

The third and current version of the ban bars all students from North Korea and Syria from applying for student visas unless they obtain waivers. Nationals of the other affected countries are eligible to apply for student visas, though in practice they may have difficulty obtaining them.

In addition to the statistical data, attitudes of international students applying to U.S. universities indicate a level of fear and apprehension. Higher education institutions are reporting that the social and political environment continues to be a challenge for international recruitment (Redden, 2018a). Although there are many variables that impact international enrollments, the drop in new international students comes at a time when many in international education have expressed fears that Trump's rhetoric and policies could discourage some international students from enrolling in U.S. institutions (Redden, 2018a). Among institutions that responded to the survey, 68% cited the visa application process or visa denials and delays as a reason for declining new enrollments, up 35 percentage points from last year, and 57% cited the social and political environment in the United States, up 41 percentage points from last year (IIE, 2018). Other factors cited included the cost of tuition and fees, cited by 57% of respondents, and competition from universities in other countries, cited by 54% of respondents (IIE, 2018).

The travel ban excludes those who have a "bona fide relationship" with an entity in the United States from the terms of the ban. In its June 26, 2017, order, the Supreme Court identified the following circumstances relevant to academic institutions that would qualify as a bona fide relationship: (a) a student from a designated country who has been admitted to a university, (b) a worker who has accepted an offer of employment from an American company, and (c) a lecturer invited to address an American audience (*Trump v. International Refugee Assistance Project,* 2017a). The Supreme Court's explanation of a bona fide relationship was not expanded in its 2018 ruling and therefore still holds. Though students who have been accepted to or are already enrolled in an academic institution are theoretically excluded from the travel ban because they have a "bona fide relationship" with the United States, this has proven not to be the case in practice. Many students have been caught in limbo with dire life-altering consequences.

There have been a number of reported cases of Muslim students who have not been allowed to enter or reenter the United States after traveling abroad. One such reported case is that of Ahmed Dardir, a PhD candidate in Middle East studies at Columbia University who as of February 1, 2018, has been unable to return after having finished writing his dissertation in Cairo (Redden, 2018b). Though Egypt is not one of the countries listed in any of the travel bans, current or previous, Dardir was reportedly stopped by U.S. immigration officers on a layover on his way from Egypt to JFK airport. After two rounds of interrogations, the valid visa stamp on his passport was crossed out and he was asked to sign a statement to the effect that Homeland Security could not establish that he was entering the United States for nonimmigration purposes; he was asked to withdraw his visa. Though he pointed repeatedly to the paperwork proving his university affiliation, he was refused admittance on the flight and had his visa revoked. Dardir has since applied for another visa, which, as of February 2018, was still being subjected to an additional layer of review common for applicants from the Middle East, known as "administrative processing." Dardir states that

> While on the short term I may be able to defend online, this has greatly impacted my ability to apply for jobs in the U.S., or to be able to travel to the U.S. for conferences or workshops. Given the centrality of U.S. universities to academia, and the general dearth of academic positions, this puts me in a very difficult situation. (Redden, 2018b, para. 39)

After struggling with the impossible choice of pursuing academic dreams or having the ability to see family and loved ones back home, other students have been forced to choose to attend academic institutions outside of the United States. Faraj Aljarih, a Libyan graduate student at Washington State University, was interviewed by *Inside Higher Ed* after the initial travel ban was issued in January of 2017 (Redden, 2018b). At the time, he was a student in a master's program at Washington State University, where he wanted to stay for his PhD. He had not visited his family in Libya for a number of years and was grappling with the possibility of not seeing them for many more years. At that time, Executive Order 13,769 prohibited Aljarih from returning if he left the United States. Proclamation 9,654, unlike the first, technically allows Libyans to come to the United States on nonimmigrant student visas but Aljarih had decided not to live in that limbo; he stated,

> I was hoping to pursue my Ph.D. at WSU, but I had to leave the country to see my family after four years of doing master's in the States. . . . I got admitted to the Ph.D. program at the University of Ottawa, in Canada. Their visa process is much easier, and I will be able to visit my family here in Libya on holidays and school breaks. (quoted in Redden, 2018b, para. 3)

Although some students are forced to abandon dreams of studying in the United States, others make the impossible choice of not seeing their families for a potentially indefinite period of time. Though the current ban technically allows for visas of close family members such as parents, the delayed processing times and increased scrutiny has prolonged visa issuance and resulted in families being separated during the most crucial times—marriages, births, and even funerals. Leila Zonouzi, an Iranian graduate student in the Global Studies Department of University of California, Santa Barbara (UCSB), was unable to have her in-laws attend her wedding because they were under "administrative processing" after almost a year (as quoted in Spence, 2018, para. 11). Some of her friends "went through childbirth without their mothers holding their hands" (as quoted in Spence, 2018, para. 15). Many "are forced to choose between risking their degrees and missing family emergencies or their loved ones' funerals. . . . Having to make that choice deliberately makes it all the more painful" (as quoted in Spence, 2018, para. 19). Zonouzi feels her "story is a droplet in an ocean of misfortune. . . . [You] truly feel like you're being treated as 'less than' just because your birth place is in the wrong geographical zone" (as quoted in Spence, 2018, para. 28).

Even when students make the difficult decision to stay in the United States and forego seeing family, they find that their opportunities for research, attending conferences, and even job prospects have become severely constricted. Many students are unable to apply to positions outside the United States because the process includes interviews at the international institution; if students travel to their interviews, they fear not being able to return to the United States (Spence, 2018). "We miss out on so many opportunities," explains UCSB electrical engineering graduate student Maryam Rasekh (as quoted in Spence, 2018, para. 6). Iranian nationals are usually issued single-entry visas to the United States and risk not being issued return visas if they travel outside. They cannot attend conferences outside the United States, which Rasekh acknowledges as having delayed the progress of her work considerably as "many times the relevant conferences . . . [are] outside [of] the U.S." (as quoted in Spence, 2018, para. 10).

Impacts on U.S. Academia as a Whole

The intellectual contributions and diverse cultural perspectives that international students bring to U.S. campuses are invaluable. There is great concern over the impact of the Muslim ban on academia and scholarship more broadly. By attracting students of different cultures and religions, universities accomplish their educational mission of fostering open and dynamic discussion while teaching local students about the greater world. Cross-cultural exchanges and collaborations have long been a bedrock of higher learning in the United States and one of the primary reasons for our economic growth and our position as a global innovator—relying on diversity of knowledge, points of view, and scholarship to advance our own country and the world.

Administrators fear that schools will be adversely impacted financially, academically, and culturally. Financially, schools will likely see a marked decrease in the out-of-state tuition paid by foreign students at the nation's public colleges, both from students who are banned from the United States and from others who are distressed by the ban or who choose to study in other English-speaking countries that are perceived as more welcoming. Academically, losing contact with certain regions could limit the production of new knowledge, intercultural collaboration, and cutting-edge innovation. But even more important in certain ways "there's this sort of isolation in terms of the cultural context and that has implications for cultural understanding," stated Joanna Regulska (as quoted in Deryu, 2017, para. 9), the vice provost and associate chancellor for global affairs at University of California, Davis. Not every U.S. student has the time or ability to go abroad; only 10% currently do, and having a diverse international student body allows American students to gain cultural and religious understanding that benefits them as well as the United States as a whole (Deryu, 2017).

Academic institutions in the United States are among the most favored and attractive destinations for international students, the leading two reasons being the quality of education and the traditional U.S. welcoming climate—which is now seen to be changing drastically. An IIE survey found that concern about international student yield is widespread among institutions of higher learning in the United States. It found that institutions were most highly concerned about whether admitted students from the Middle East will arrive on campus in the fall of 2018 (IIE, 2017). Securing and maintaining a visa is reported as the top concern among these students, with nearly 50% of higher education institutions sharing the same concern as students (IIE, 2017). Feeling welcome in the United States was an almost equal concern, with 41% of institutions noting so from their conversations with prospective students (IIE, 2017).

In response to the issuance of the first travel ban, schools across the country sent notes of support to faculty and students in an effort to provide comfort and information. The president of Princeton University, Christopher Eisgruber, reflected on his own family in his statement:

> Princeton's position on immigration policy issues reflects our conviction that every single person on this campus has benefited from the ability of people to cross borders in search of learning or a better life. That is emphat-

ically true for me. My mother and her family arrived in this country as refugees escaping from a war-torn continent. They would have perished had they been denied visas. My father first came to America as an exchange student from a country that had recently been at war with the United States, and he then studied at Purdue University as a foreign graduate student. (Princeton Office of Communication, 2017, para. 6)

President Eisgruber joined with other university presidents to create an Alliance on Higher Education and Immigration (Gilbert, 2017). The alliance is dedicated to increasing public understanding of how immigration policies and practices affect students, campuses, and communities (Gilbert, 2017). The group supports policies that create a welcoming environment for immigrant, undocumented, and international students on American campuses (Gilbert, 2017).

John DeGioia (2017), the president of Georgetown University, focused on shared religious values:

Our Catholic and Jesuit identity provides the foundation for our lives together. Guided by our mission, we have placed a special emphasis on interreligious dialogue and our openness to different faith traditions and cultures. This includes our efforts to support a diverse and vibrant Muslim community on campus. (para. 6)

In recognition of the severe adverse impacts, public universities have been involved in legal challenges to the bans, and their arguments about the negative effects of the travel restrictions on their ability to recruit international students and scholars have been important in helping states that have brought the legal cases establish standing to sue.

Financially, the travel ban could have a severe chilling effect, costing U.S. universities hundreds of millions of dollars a year. One survey shows students from the six original banned countries alone bring in more than $500 million to the U.S. economy each year (Carapezza, 2017). In response to the travel ban, international students are more reluctant to apply to the United States and are instead applying to places like Canada, the United Kingdom, Australia, and New Zealand, where they don't fear having to face the same discrimination and hostility (Carapezza, 2017). These other English-speaking countries are in turn attempting to attract the impacted international students to their institutions. The Canadian government is providing millions of dollars to attract the best and brightest scientists and innovators from around the world. "The international market is very lively. It's very competitive," says Bruce Dowton, president of Macquarie University in Sydney (as quoted in Carapezza, 2017, para. 15). Dowton says there has been a 30%

uptick in international applications since Trump's election. "We certainly look to provide an attractive offering for students to come to Macquarie, and I know other university presidents around Australia see it the same way" (as quoted in Carapezza, 2017, para. 17).

If U.S. schools admit students who are later blocked from the country, universities could lose a lot. "Our institutions are very concerned," says Melanie Gottlieb, deputy director at American Association of Collegiate Registrars and Admissions Officers (AACRAO) (as quoted in Carapezza, 2017, para. 9). Four of 10 of the colleges that responded have seen a drop in global applications. Nearly 80% expressed concerns about application yield (Carapezza, 2017).

Though the travel ban itself affects relatively few countries, many in higher education are concerned that a perception among international students that the United States is unwelcoming or unsafe and uncertainty about visa policies could be contributing factors to a drop in international enrollments at U.S. universities, the first such drop in many years. A National Science Foundation report documented a 2.2% decline in international undergraduate enrollment and a 5.5% decline in international graduate enrollment at American colleges and universities in fall 2017, compared to fall 2016 (National Science Board, 2018). A Council of Graduate Schools survey found a 16% decline in the number of new students from Iran (Okahana & Zhou, 2018).

There is a clear recognition that, academically, U.S. institutions will be severely disadvantaged by the travel ban. Higher education, academia, and especially science and technology disciplines have been almost unanimous in their opposition to the travel bans, which university leaders and associations have characterized as harmful to free exchange and scholarly collaboration (Redden, 2018b). Rush Holt, CEO of the American Association for the Advancement of Science (AAAS), said

> If indeed science is to benefit people, economically, culturally, personally, and if you want the research enterprise to thrive, you have to pay attention to the basic principles of the free exchange of ideas and the free exchange of people and the ability to collaborate. (quoted in Redden, 2018b, para. 19)

Various organizations are reporting different degrees of impact on their meetings. AAAS was unable to host one of its award recipients in February 2017 after the first travel ban had been issued (Redden, 2018b). Rania Abdelhameed, an electrical engineer at Sudan University of Science and Technology, received one of five Women in Science Elsevier Foundation Awards but was not able to attend the meeting and had her award bestowed remotely (Redden, 2018b). Four other individuals were not able to attend the 2017 AAAS Annual Meeting due to visa policy, either because they were from one of the countries targeted or because they had concerns about the policy (Redden, 2018b). One of those individuals, Mohamed Hassan from Sudan, was executive director of the World Academy of Sciences at the time (Redden, 2018b). The Middle East Studies Association, which has been involved in one of the court cases challenging the travel bans, reported an effect of the travel restrictions on participation levels at its November conference in Washington (Redden, 2018b). Registration was down by about 400 people (Redden, 2018b). Attendance is typically around 2,400 people and in 2017 it was less than 2,000. Membership was down by roughly 250 members (Redden, 2018b).

In addition to those who are restricted from traveling to the United States and other Muslims who are not traveling for fear of a hostile and discriminatory climate, there is a third group of academics and scholars who are not Muslim and are not restricted but are choosing not to come to the United States due to their view of the ban as a human rights violation. After the initial travel ban was announced, an online petition calling for a boycott of U.S.-based academic conferences garnered thousands of signatures. Gustau Catalán, a research professor at the Catalan Institute of Nanoscience and Nanotechnology in Barcelona, decided to boycott conferences in the United States:

> My rationale then, which continues now, and which I have told to the [three institutions] inviting me, was the following: I am not happy attending a conference where, had I been a citizen of a 'wrong' country, I would not have been allowed to enter. It is not fair. (as quoted in Redden, 2018a, para. 23)

Such boycotts put research and innovation in jeopardy globally and also impact the interchange of knowledge and progress furthered by global conferences; it puts international academics in a very difficult position: "By opting out of the U.S., I am opting out of the main events to showcase my research" (as quoted in Redden, 2018a, para. 23).

Proposed Ways Forward

Given the immense amount of fear and confusion among students, as well as the severe implications of the Muslim travel ban on campuses that champion nondiscrimination and values consistent with human rights standards, it becomes imperative for academic institutions in the United States to support their students, faculty, and the greater society through concrete and practical steps.

Most importantly, academic institutions should develop strong policies and procedures to provide support, guidance, and at times comfort to impacted students, their families, and the broader campus community who may be dealing with fear and anxiety as a result of the travel bans and related rhetoric and actions. The undeniably anti-immigrant sentiment of the travel bans, as well as Trump's rhetoric about the bans, Muslims, and immigrants in general, has led to a heightened level of fear and confusion among international students and their families, particularly Muslim students. There is an existing perception among prospective international students and their families that the United States is no longer a safe and welcoming environment for them. Safety and security is a priority for any university student, and many families are fearful for their children applying to U.S. academic institutions where they might face hostility due to their religion or ethnic background.

Another important step for academic institutions is to develop clear guidelines for international students regarding the application process, making particular note of timelines that encourage early application. Schools should consider setting up extra support services for international students from the impacted countries and the broader region, as well as Muslim students who are likely to have extra concerns related to the application process. Schools should provide clear information about the forms students need to fill out, consular office visits, and what the current interview process may look like. Often, when students are not prepared for consular interviews, their visas could be denied and they could potentially be barred from future entry to the United States.

Schools also need to create policies and procedures for informing impacted students on visa terms, rights, potential violations, and how to seek redress. Schools should set up offices to provide support and assistance to impacted students and help navigate any visa or immigration-related issues that could come up. Many universities have strengthened their law school immigrants' rights programs and/or set up additional legal support through offices of international students' affairs or the universities' legal counsel's offices to assist impacted students in knowing, supporting, and being able to advocate for their rights.

Universities can creatively work to address challenges while remaining committed to ensuring that impacted students from "banned countries" are not banned from access to higher education opportunities. By (a) developing clear policies reaffirming their commitment to upholding international human rights standards; (b) implementing guidelines and extra support services instructing international students from the banned countries on the university application procedures as well as visa and immigration procedures; and (c) setting up mental health and social support services on campus for international students and Muslim students dealing with fear about campus climate or general anti-immigrant and anti-Muslim rhetoric. Universities can play a crucial role in continuing to attract, enroll, and retain the diverse international students who have benefited our country throughout its history, using their abilities, creativity, and drive to enhance the quality of students, faculty, and staff at institutions of higher learning and the broader society.

Discussion Questions

1. What do you think a university's role should be in upholding or promoting international human rights?
2. How do you think a campus is impacted by the types of international students who are able to attend? Have you seen any differences on your campuses since the enactment of the travel bans?
3. What is a university's responsibility to maintain or promote a diverse international student body? Does it have such a responsibility? Why or why not?
4. What are other ways universities could be involved in addressing the travel ban and/or its impacts? Are there other steps, other than those suggested in this chapter, that universities should take?

References

Carapezza, K. (2017, April 7). Travel ban's "chilling effect" could cost universities hundreds of millions. *NPR*. Retrieved from https://www.npr.org/sections/ed/2017/04/07/522773429/travel-bans-chilling-effect-could-cost-universities-hundreds-of-millions

Dakwar, J. (2017, February 2). All international laws Trump's Muslim ban is breaking. *Al Jazeera*. Retrieved from https://www.aljazeera.com/indepth/opinion/2017/02/international-laws-trump-muslim-ban-breaking-170202135132664.html

DeGioia, J. (2017, January 29). *Regarding our international students, staff, and faculty.* Retrieved from https://president.georgetown.edu/message-immigration-jan-2017

Deryu, E. (2017, January 30). How Trump's immigration order is affecting higher education. *Atlantic*. Retrieved from https://www.theatlantic.com/education/archive/2017/01/how-trumps-muslim-immigration-order-could-affect-higher-education/514925/

Dobunzinskis, A. (2017, January 28). "I got handcuffed and just started crying"—Sudanese student describes US detention. *Reuters*. Retrieved from https://www.reuters.com/article/usa-trump-immigration-detention/i-got-handcuffed-

and-just-started-crying-sudanese-student-describes-u-s-detention-idINKBN-15D0AU

Exec. Order No. 13,769, 82 Fed. Reg. 8977 (2017a).

Exec. Order No. 13,780, 82 Fed. Reg. 13209 (2017b).

Farrugia, C., & Andrejko, N. (2018). New student international enrollment, 2006/07–2016/17. *Open doors: Report on international education exchange.* Retrieved from https://www.iie.org/Research-and-Insights/Open-Doors/Data/International-Students/Enrollment

Gilbert, R. (2017, December 13). President Eisgruber joins university leaders nationwide to found Presidents' Alliance on Higher Education and Immigration. *Daily Princetonian.* Retrieved from http://www.dailyprincetonian.com/article/2017/12/eisgruber-presidents-alliance-on-higher-education-and-immigration

Hawaii v. Trump, No. 17-15589 (9th Cir. 2017).

Institute of International Education (IIE). (2017, July). *Shifting tides? Understanding international student yield for fall 2017.* Washington, DC: IIE Center for Academic Mobility Research and Impact.

Trump v. International Refugee Assistance Project, No. 17-1351 (4th Cir. May 25, 2017a).

Trump v. International Refugee Assistance Project, 582 U.S. _____ (2017b).

Johnson, J. (2015, December 7). Trump calls for "total and complete shutdown of Muslims entering the United States." *Washington Post.* Retrieved from https://www.washingtonpost.com/news/post-politics/wp/2015/12/07/donald-trump-calls-for-total-and-complete-shutdown-of-muslims-entering-the-united-states/

Korematsu v. United States, 323 U.S. 214 (1944).

National Science Board. (2018). *Science and engineering indicators 2018.* Alexandria, VA: National Science Foundation. Retrieved from https://www.nsf.gov/statistics/2018/nsb20181/assets/nsb20181.pdf

Okahana, H., & Zhou, E. (2018). *International graduate applications and enrollment: Fall 2017.* Washington, D.C.: Council of Graduate Schools. Retrieved from https://cgsnet.org/ckfinder/userfiles/files/Intl_Survey_Report_Fall2017.pdf

Princeton Office of Communication. (2017, January 29). President Eisgruber issues statement on federal immigration executive order [Press release]. Retrieved from https://www.princeton.edu/news/2017/01/29/president-eisgruber-issues-statement-federal-immigration-executive-order

Proclamation No. 9645, 82 Fed. Reg. 45161 (September 24, 2017).

Redden, E. (2018a, November 13). New international enrollments decline again. *Inside Higher Ed.* Retrieved from https://www.insidehighered.com/news/2018/11/13/new-international-student-enrollments-continue-decline-us-universities

Redden, E. (2018b, February 1). A year of travel bans. *Inside Higher Ed.* Retrieved from https://www.insidehighered.com/news/2018/02/01/year-later-trump-administrations-travel-restrictions-opposed-many-higher-ed-are

Refugee Act of 1980, Pub. L 96-212, 94 Stat. 102.

Spence, E. (2018, January 25). Students still strained by travel ban 1 year later. *Daily Nexus*. Retrieved from http://dailynexus.com/2018-01-25/students-still-strained-by-travel-ban-1-year-later/

State of Hawaii v. Trump, 263 F. Supp.3d 1049 (D. Ha. 2017).

State of Washington and State of Minnesota v. Trump, 847 F.3d 1151 (9th Cir. 2017).

Trump lifts travel ban on Chad. (2018, April 11). *BBC News*. Retrieved from https://www.bbc.com/news/world-africa-43724045

Trump v. Hawaii, 565 U.S. ____ (2018).

United Nations, Charter of the United Nations, 24 October 1945, 1 UNTS XVI, available at: https://www.refworld.org/docid/3ae6b3930.html [accessed 3 December 2019]

UN Committee on the Elimination of Racial Discrimination (CERD). *Report of the Committee on the Elimination of Racial Discrimination*, New York, 2004, Supplement No. 18 (A/59/18) at p. 44.

UN General Assembly. Convention Against Torture and Other Cruel, Inhuman or Degrading Treatment or Punishment, 10 December 1984, United Nations, Treaty Series, vol. 1465, p. 114.

UN General Assembly. Convention Relating to the Status of Refugees, 28 July 1951, United Nations, Treaty Series, vol. 189, p. 137.

UN General Assembly. International Convention on the Elimination of All Forms of Racial Discrimination, 21 December 1965, United Nations, Treaty Series, vol. 660, p. 195.

UN General Assembly. International Covenant on Civil and Political Rights, 16 December 1966, United Nations, Treaty Series, vol. 999, p. 171.

UN General Assembly. Universal Declaration of Human Rights, 10 December 1948, 217 A (III).

UN High Commissioner for Refugees (UNHCR). Advisory Opinion on the Extraterritorial Application of Non-Refoulement Obligations Under the 1951 Convention Relating to the Status of Refugees and its 1967 Protocol, 26 January 2007.

UN High Commissioner for Refugees (UNHCR). The 1951 Convention Relating to the Status of Refugees and Its 1967 Protocol, September 2011.

UN High Commissioner for Refugees (UNHCR). Joint IOM-UNHCR Statement on President Trump's Refugee Order, 28 January 2017.

UN UDHR. (2015, October 6). *History of the document*. Retrieved from https://https://www.unhcr.org/en-us/news/press/2017/1/588bc4e34/joint-iom-unhcr-statement-president-trumps-refugee-order.html

U.S. Const. art. II, § 2, cl. 2.

U.S. Const. art. VI, cl. 2.

US expands travel ban to include North Korea. (2017, September 25). *BBC News*. Retrieved from https://www.bbc.com/news/world-us-canada-41382585

4

IMMIGRANT STATUS
OF MUSLIMS

Bo Lee and Shafiqa Ahmadi

A look into the history of U.S. immigration policies reveals the power of laws to create politicized identities through exclusivity and control. Immigration law limits who gets to come into the United States and creates belonging through immigration status (Ajrouch & Jamal, 2007). These policies are one of the primary means by which identity is established in America. The design of immigration laws in the United States centers Whiteness in citizenship and otherizes migrant identities and experiences, placing groups of individuals into a hierarchy of belonging (King, 2002). These laws confirm concepts of belonging to be synonymous to Whiteness as an American social and cultural norm, thus pushing forward a political agenda where other identities are not only shaped but also controlled by the legal system. The history of immigration law reveals how policies now have transcended racialized exclusion and paved the path to normalize discriminatory policies to criminalize, track, and diminish civil rights of Muslims as an American defense policy. This construction of a politicized identity of Muslims further reinforces negative stereotypes of Muslims in the United States (McCloud, 2006). Muslim college students are burdened with navigating and negotiating not only stereotypes but also immigration laws' and policies' direct impact on their higher education opportunities and learning experiences. In an effort to better understand how U.S. immigration laws and policies impact Muslims, this chapter will address (a) the history of immigration law in the United States, (b) Muslims and Muslim immigrants and refugees, (c) the impact of immigration law and policies on Muslim students in higher education, and (d) recommendations for policy and practice. This chapter concludes with a set of questions for class discussion.

History of Immigration Law

The U.S. immigration system begins at the start of the republic with the migration of European settlers and the forced migration of slave laborers (Magee, 2010). During this time, White colonists actively recruited people for mass immigration to the United States from European countries and simultaneously forced migration of people from African countries (Schuck, 1984). The United States federally endorsed and regulated American transatlantic slavery importation practices for artificially free labor—thus creating the first major pillar of the immigration system embedded in racialization in the United States (Schuck, 1984).

In 1790, the first law legalizing the right to naturalization established requirements for citizenship, creating restrictions on belonging in the United States. The 1790 Naturalization Act specified eligibility for citizenship to "free white persons" with two years of residence in the country and demonstration of "good moral character" (Cohn, 2015, para. 2). Citizenship provides a right to work, travel, organize, own property, vote, and many other freedoms. This act inaugurated the legal status of belonging in the United States. Through this status, a hierarchy of belonging was created by excluding indigenous peoples of the United States and persons of African descent, centering White immigrants as American.

By the 1800s, the United States was rapidly urbanizing with the Industrial Revolution; meanwhile, opposition to the slave trade was popularizing in colonizing countries (Schuck, 1984). As a result of the increase in dissent, the Act of 1807 was instituted, banning the importation of slaves from Africa (Martin, 2008). By legally enacting this immigration policy, the rule created protections for African peoples from forced migration and directly regularized the criminality of the slave trade. Though the Act of 1807 prohibited forced migration, slavery was still legal and laws restricting eligibility for citizenship remained the same, limiting persons of African heritage as quasi-citizen-workers (Schuck, 1984). Immigration status reinforced a racial hierarchy of belonging. It wasn't until the end of the Civil War in 1865 that slavery was abolished with the enactment of the Thirteenth Amendment. In 1868, the ratification of the Fourteenth Amendment extended naturalization to peoples of African descent but still limited those same rights for indigenous peoples (U.S. Const. amend. XIV).

Ethnic, cultural, and class composition of the immigrant population was changing dramatically in the 1880s as a wave of "new" immigrants came from different European regions to the south and east as well as the "Orient" (Schuck, 2018). This change engendered racial and religious prejudice; class conflict; and fear of divergent political, social, and cultural ideologies threatening "Americanism" (Schuck, 2018). Starting in 1875, new exclusionary immigration laws were introduced, targeting new racial groups. The Chinese Exclusion Act in 1882 and Geary Act of 1892 ended free immigration, with a ban on Chinese laborers immigrating to the United States, legalization of deportation and/or imprisonment of unauthorized Chinese immigrants, and restriction of residing Chinese immigrants from naturalizing (Cohn, 2015). Simultaneously, the Immigration Act of 1882 was enacted, establishing the first federal oversight of immigration by screening arriving passengers and denying access to land (Migration Policy Institute, 2013). These laws were an expansion of government power to control identities through immigration and lawfully exercise punitive repercussion. The rules subscribed racialization in America, creating levels of otherness and normalizing the alienation of everyone deviant from those in power and "White Americanism" through control. As a result, immigration policies can serve as powerful civil rights laws for vulnerable peoples as they have power to control identity and belonging through citizenship status.

The 1900s set forth a geopolitical agenda of *restrictive nationalism* to maintain power and control in upholding "Americanism" (Lee, 2007). A series of migrant policies was legislated regulating immigration according to considerations of national interest, sovereignty, and power (Schuck, 1984). The Immigration Act of 1903 became the first law to restrict immigration based on immigrants' political beliefs, banning anarchists among others. Then in 1917, based on racial prejudice such as the "Yellow Peril" and "Asian Menace," the Asiatic Barred Zone Act was instituted. The legislation banned immigration from most Asian countries and almost all of the Middle East. The only exemptions were students and skilled professionals and their families (Migration Policy Institute, 2013). The law also required all immigrants over 16 to demonstrate basic reading ability. The law significantly restricted entry into the United States, establishing the most aggressive agenda to exclude others from the national vision of America, and set the precedent for exceptionalism and model minorities as requisites for entry and adaptation into the United States became increasingly elite.

In 1921 and enhanced in 1924, the Emergency Quota Act and National Origins Quota Act established numerically limited admission based on nationality (Cohn, 2015). The Quota Board created census race categories to make calculations for immigration limitations. These two laws aimed to restore earlier immigration patterns, favoring migration from Northern and Western European countries and limiting migration from Eastern and Southern Europe and Asia (Cohn, 2015). This set of laws explicitly controlled population and ranked them through quotas in a hierarchy of desirability and belonging in the United States (Schuck, 1984). Moreover, the law pushed forward a shared sense of Whiteness among Europeans that allowed direct pathways to "becoming American." However, non-European immigrants, among them Japanese, Chinese, Mexicans, and Filipinos, were racialized into national origins, rendering their identities unalterably foreign and unassimilable to the nation (Schuck, 1984).

After the catastrophic events of World War I, the Great Depression, and World War II, political, social, and geopolitical factors shifted America's immigration policies across the world. In 1942, a bilateral agreement between the United States and Mexico, called the Bacero Agreement, permitted Mexican nationals to serve as temporary agricultural workers during World War II labor shortages. Latin Americans were not subject to numerical quotas; however, immigration laws came through a form of restrictive measures at the southern borders with the creation of the Border Patrol through the Department of Labor, criminalization of unlawful entry, and tightening admission eligibility requirements (Schuck, 2018). Although immigration law served as an entryway to become American for White immigrants, immigration policies for Latin Americans served as a political and economic strategy and benefit for labor in America's economy. Moreover, employee protections and visas were not laid out until the late twentieth century with the Illegal Immigration Reform and Immigrant Responsibility Act (IIRIRA), which laid out its purpose to increase enforcement and establish work site enforcement to remove "criminals and other deportable aliens" (Immigration and Naturalization Service, 1997). These immigration laws ignited the rhetoric of Latin American immigrants as strangers, objects of vigilance and suspicion, confirming otherness as an American social and cultural norm (Schuck, 1984). For Asian Americans, new legislation in 1952 finally allowed a limited number of Asian immigrants to enter the United States again and race was formally removed as grounds for exclusion. With more time, the Immigration and Nationality Act of 1962 was passed, creating a new system favoring family reunification and skilled immigrants, rather than country quotas and increased admission eligibility requirements (Cohn, 2015). Immigration law thus sets a standard of exceptionalism for "Orient" immigrants. This standard places the legal system as the institution for shaping and controlling assimilation. The results of this legal-cultural process casts Latin Americans as "illegal aliens" and Asians as permanent foreigners (Schuck, 2018).

From 1948 to the 1990s, a series of refugee legislation was established to address the refugee crisis of individuals displaced from their homelands by Nazi persecution, the destruction of World War II, religious and political persecution, and effects of the Cold War and Vietnam War with opposition to Soviet-sponsored regimes such as those in Afghanistan and Cuba (Bockley, 1995). Through pressure from the international community with the growing refugee crises from the multiple wars in which the United States was centered, the government employed reactive, exclusionary, and prohibitive refugee policies. By enacting rigorous eligibility requirements and responding using defense mechanisms regarding the wars it participated in, the United States set forth a precedent in integrating immigration law as part of American defense policy.

Immigration Laws and Policies and the Muslim Community

Although immigration laws and policies were always applicable to Muslims, 9/11 was a watershed moment in American history that put a spotlight on Muslims from various nationalities, grouping them as a monolithic entity. In 2001, policies employed in response to 9/11 instigated the beginning of America's most restrictive and politicized immigration laws. It began with the USA PATRIOT Act (2001), broadening the terrorism grounds for excluding aliens from entering the United States and increasing monitoring of foreign students. It diminished the civil liberties of Muslims and normalized discriminatory policies to track, criminalize, and diminish civil rights of Muslims as an American defense policy. Moreover, it established anti-Muslim sentiments and racialization of Muslims as phenomena post-9/11 (Ahmadi, 2011). The following year, two laws were enacted: the Enhanced Border Security and Visa Entry Reform Act (2002) and the Homeland Security Act (2002). These significantly expanded the government's policing and enforcement powers and are emblematic of Americans' willingness to exchange civil rights for safety in times of heightened fear (Ahmadi, 2011). These laws shaped, controlled, and pushed forward a politicized identity for Muslims.

The evolution of immigration law in the United States paved the path to normalize and allow discriminatory practices in immigration law. In 2017, Donald Trump issued three executive orders (the Muslim bans) that banned foreign nationals from 7 predominantly Muslim countries from visiting the country for 90 days, suspended entry to the country of all Syrian refugees indefinitely, and prohibited any other refugees from coming into the country for 120 days (American Civil Liberties Union, 2017). Citing the terrorist attacks of September 11, 2001, President Trump said the United States must protect its citizens from foreign nationals who want to commit terrorist attacks in the United States (Executive Order No. 13,769, 2017). Today, immigration law is synonymous with American defense policy, laced with hateful, discriminatory practices against the Muslim community. President Trump has further promoted a politicized identity of Muslims and further reinforced negative stereotypes of Muslims in the United States, which have dangerous repercussions in violating the civil rights of Muslims and harming millions of individuals and their families.

Immigration Law and Policies and Muslim College Students

The intersectional experiences of Muslim college students are readily visible when Muslims are racialized as a group and viewed as forever foreigners regardless of their immigration status and/or national origin. This systemic oppression strengthens American defense policy under the guise of national security. Part of the U.S.'s defense policy is to otherize the Muslim community by using Islamophobic rhetoric to distinguish between the "us" and the "other," making Muslims and individuals perceived to be Muslims or associated with Islam as the "others" (Ahmadi, 2011). On the 2016 presidential campaign trail, Trump targeted Muslims and made disparaging comments about the U.S. Muslim community as a whole. This otherization of Muslims contributed to a 17% increase in anti-Muslim bias incidents and a 15% increase in hate crimes against Muslims in 2017 as compared to those reported in 2016 (Council on American-Islamic Relations, 2018).

The Federal Bureau of Investigation (FBI) reports that during the 2016 presidential election season there was an increase in the number of hate crimes, hate speech, and incidents of bias and discrimination against Muslim, Arab, and South Asian communities. The FBI data from 2015 reveal that there was a 67% increase in hate crimes against Muslims since 2014. Within the 10 days after the 2016 election nearly 900 incidents of hate or bias were reported (Southern Poverty Law Center, 2016a). There were 1,094 incidents in the first month after the election and 1,863 between November 9, 2016, and March 31, 2017 (Southern Poverty Law Center, 2016b, 2017). According to Ahmadi, Sanchez, and Cole (2019),

> schools were a particularly common location for hate incidents with 284 at primary and secondary schools, 330 on college campuses, and 178 incidents involving the posting of White supremacist flyers. The flyers were posted in two bursts, one the week after the election and one during the month of February, and the majority of flyers were posted at colleges. (p. 104; see also Southern Poverty Law Center, 2016b, 2017).

After Trump was elected, "Muslims across the nation and across different colleges and universities were subject to discrimination, hate crimes, and harassment" (Ahmadi et al., 2019, p. 104). This type of hostile environment can impact the educational satisfaction and engagement of Muslim students. Cole and Ahmadi (2010) found that although Muslim students' academic performance did not differ from that of their Jewish and Christian counterparts, they did experience less educational satisfaction. On campus, Muslim students participated in many diversity-related activities, but they were often the educators and information providers rather than the recipients of information (Cole & Ahmadi, 2010). These findings indicate that institutions of higher education should create safe educational environments for Muslim students to engage in; moreover, Muslim students should not be forced into a position to educate their peers while going through traumatizing experiences. These experiences of otherness and isolation are further compounded when discrimination, hate crimes, and harassment are directed at international students, who often do not have support systems in place in a foreign country.

With the issuance of the Muslim ban and the subsequent Supreme Court decision to uphold the third version of the ban, both domestic and international students and faculty at higher education institutions across the country and world are negatively impacted (Ahmadi et al., 2019). In 2015–2016, over 12,000 Iranian students studied in the United States. These numbers will change, not only because of the Muslim bans but also because of the current (July 2019) political climate featuring talk of the United States going to war with Iran. Royall & Company conducted a survey between the first and second Muslim bans of prospective international students from 150 countries to better understand whether the Trump administration had impacted the students' desire to study in the United States (Royall & Dodson, 2017). The survey found that out of 2,000 international students, nearly 1 in 3 students had less interest in studying in the United States because of the current political climate (Royall & Dodson, 2017). Almost 69% stated that they had "concerns about the U.S. presidential administration" (Royall & Dodson, 2017, p. 10). The other top reasons for less interest in studying in the United States included worries about travel restrictions, safety concerns, cost, and prejudice or discrimination (Royall & Dodson, 2017). Out of the 2,000 students surveyed, only 16 students were from 1 of the 6 countries listed in the Muslim bans, which illustrates that the Muslim bans and overall political climate are influencing international students' views about the United States in general (Royall & Dodson, 2017). According to Carapezza (2017), "Students from those six countries [listed in the Muslim ban] alone bring in more than $500 million to the U.S. economy each year" (para. 7). The significance of the Muslim bans, Islamophobic rhetoric, and the promotion of a politicized identity for Muslims in general and Muslim college students specifically has implications for policy and practice for higher education administrators, faculty, and students as they support and protect Muslim students in postsecondary institutions.

Recommendations

Higher education institutions are purported to be intellectual spaces where students are encouraged to engage in free dialogue and exchange of ideas. For Muslim students, however, free dialogue and exchange of ideas and the right to freely assemble and associate are curtailed due to the current political rhetoric and immigration laws and policies, such as the Muslim ban, that contribute to a hostile campus climate. In an effort to better understand immigration laws' and policies' impact on domestic and international Muslim college students, address Islamophobia in higher education, combat discrimination, and create understanding, postsecondary institutions should consider the following:

- Counter Islamophobia by providing professional development for staff, students, and faculty and systematically training the campus community through information, education, and empowering institutional leaders to be knowledgeable about religious identity, student development, and diversity that impact campus climate positively and negatively. This type of training will combat the negative impact of stereotypes portrayed in the media about Muslims and increase security and support for Muslim students on college campuses (Will, 2015).
- Invite Muslim American leaders and speakers to campuses, conferences, interfaith events, and panels, as an essential step for students, staff, and faculty to alleviate the burden placed on Muslim students, who often become the educators. According to McCollum, citing Pew Research Center (2017) report, over 50% of Americans neither know nor have met a person who identifies as Muslim. Higher education leaders and student affairs professionals should transform fear of "the other" into opportunity and challenge stereotypes through education, information, and intercultural and interreligious community-building (Kunst, Thomsen, & Sam, 2014).
- Provide more opportunities for faculty and scholars to conduct more research to better understand the extent to which religious diversity impacts campus culture, climate, and the critical link between educational satisfaction and Muslim students'

diversity-related engagement (Ahmadi, Cole, & Prado, 2018). Student affairs professionals and faculty could enrich and have a substantive impact on Muslim students' educational outcomes through positive reinforcement and facilitating the development of Muslim students' religious and spiritual identity (Cole & Ahmadi, 2010).

- Create and support identity, religious/spiritual, and multicultural centers for Muslim college students, particularly now when Muslim college students are negatively impacted by the current political climate, immigration laws, and policies. Institutions that support multicultural and identity centers and student-run organizations have helped reduce anti-Muslim sentiments on college campuses by addressing stereotypes and increasing contact with students of various backgrounds (Asfari, 2017). In order to create understanding these "centers allow for students of diverse backgrounds to connect and interact with each other, identifying shared values and commonalities" (Ahmadi et al., 2018, p. 20). This type of exposure helps individuals develop respect for differences and creates understanding through knowledge (Asfari, 2017). Additionally, these centers can provide a safe space for Muslim students to express themselves, share their experiences, develop campus relationships, and build community (Seggie & Sanford, 2010).

- Create anonymous reporting mechanisms and a safe space where Muslim students can report incidents of prejudice and discrimination, which can help make Muslim college students feel comfortable and supported on campus (Seggie & Sanford, 2010). Muslim college students experience macro aggressions and incidents of bigotry, which often do not rise to level of assault to be investigated. When these incidents are investigated, they are often not done properly, giving Muslim students the impression that their institution does not support them. Institutions should also track these reports to pinpoint where these incidents are more likely to occur and add safety officers to ensure security of Muslim students as well as the whole campus community.

- Address and inform both domestic and international students regarding their legal rights and issues related to travel restrictions, safety concerns, cost, and prejudice and discrimination. Trump and his administration's rhetoric, laws, policies, and practices have a negative impact on Muslim students, international students, and other campus communities. The Muslim community in general and Muslim college students specifically are targeted by Trump's overall rhetoric and laws and policies that continue to strain and promote negative actions taken against the Muslim community. As the leader of the free world, Trump's actions have lasting ramifications in this country and in the world (Ahmadi et al., 2019). As such, offices of international services and student affairs professionals should lead informational sessions related to laws and policies.

Discussion Questions

1. Given the shifting sociocultural and geopolitical landscape of immigration laws and policies such as the current Muslim bans, in what ways can postsecondary institutions be proactive in their support of students?
2. Reflect on this and other chapters in this book. How do laws intersect to affect Muslim international students?
3. What strategies can institutional leaders and agents employ to improve campus climate for international students?
4. What can faculty do in the classroom to improve international students' experiences?

References

Ahmadi, S. (2011). The erosion of civil rights: Exploring the effects of the Patriot Act on Muslims in American higher education. *Rutgers Race & the Law Review, 12*, 1–47.

Ahmadi, S., Cole, D., & Prado, M. (2018). Understanding Islamophobia on college campuses. In M. Gasman & A. C. Samayoa (Eds.), *Contemporary issues in higher education* (pp. 135–152). New York, NY: Routledge.

Ahmadi, S., Sanchez, M., & Cole, D. (2019). Protecting Muslim students' speech and expression and resisting Islamophobia. In D. L. Morgan & C. H. Davis, III (Eds.), *Student activism, politics, and campus climate in higher education* (pp. 97–111). New York, NY: Routledge.

Ajrouch, K. J., & Jamal, A. (2007). Assimilating to a white identity: The case of Arab Americans. *International Migration Review, 41*(4), 860–879.

American Civil Liberties Union. (2017). *Timeline of the Muslim ban.* Retrieved from https://www.aclu-wa.org/pages/timeline-muslim-ban

Asfari, A. (2017). *An empirical assessment of multicultural education programs in reducing islamophobia on a college campus.* ProQuest Dissertations and Theses database.

Bockley, K. (1995). A historical overview of refugee legislation: The deception of foreign policy in the land of promise. *North Carolina Journal of International Law & Commercial Regulation, 21*, 253–292.

Carapezza, K. (2017, April 17). Travel ban's "chilling effect" could cost universities hundreds of millions. *NPR*. Retrieved from https://www.npr.org/sections/ed/2017/04/07/522773429/travel-bans-chilling-effect-could-cost-universities-hundreds-of-millions

Cohn, D. (2015, September 30). *How U.S. immigration laws and rules have changed through history*. Retrieved from https://www.pewresearch.org/fact-tank/2015/09/30/how-u-s-immigration-laws-and-rules-have-changed-through-history/

Cole, D., & Ahmadi, S. (2010). Reconsidering campus diversity: An examination of Muslim students' experiences. *The Journal of Higher Education, 81*(2), 121–139.

Council on American-Islamic Relations. (2018). *Targeted: 2018 civil rights report*. Washington, DC: Author.

Enhanced Border Security and Visa Entry Reform Act of 2002, Pub. L. No. 107-173. (2001). https://www.congress.gov/bill/107th-congress/house-bill/3525

Executive Order No. 13,769, 3 C.F.R. (2017).

Gualtieri, S. (2001). Becoming "White": Race, religion and the foundations of Syrian/Lebanese ethnicity in the United States. *Journal of American Ethnic History, 20*(4), 29–58. Retrieved from http://www.jstor.org/stable/27502745

Homeland Security Act of 2002, Pub. L. No. 107-296, 116 Stat. 2135 (2002). https://www.dhs.gov/sites/default/files/publications/hr_5005_enr.pdf

Immigration and Naturalization Service. (1997). *The triennial comprehensive report on immigration executive summary background*. Washington, DC: United States Citizenship and Immigration Services.

King, D. (2002). *Making Americans: Immigration, race and the origins of the diverse democracy*. Cambridge, MA: Harvard University Press.

Kunst, J. R., Thomsen, L., & Sam, D. L. (2014). Late Abrahamic reunion? Religious fundamentalism negatively predicts dual Abrahamic group categorization among Muslims and Christians. *European Journal of Social Psychology, 44*(4), 337–348.

Lee, E. (2007). The "Yellow Peril" and Asian exclusion in the Americas. *Pacific Historical Review, 76*(4), 537–562.

Migration Policy Institute. (2013). *Major U.S. Immigration laws, 1790–present* [Fact Sheet]. Retrieved from https://www.migrationpolicy.org/research/timeline-1790

Magee, R. V. (2010). Slavery as immigration. *Immigration and Nationality Law Review, 31*, 743–776.

Martin, M. (2008). End of slave trade meant new normal for America. *NPR*. Retrieved from https://www.npr.org/templates/story/story.php?storyId=17988106

McCloud, A. B. (2006). *Transnational Muslims in American society*. Gainesville, FL: University Press of Florida.

Pew Research Center. (2017, February 15). *Americans express increasingly warm feelings toward religious groups*. Retrieved from https://www.pewforum.org/2017/02/15/americans-express-increasingly-warm-feelings-toward-religious-groups/

Royall, P. K., & Dodson, A. (2017). Effect of the current political environment on international student enrollment. EAB. Retrieved from https://sites.psu.edu/fstern/files/2016/04/Fstern_-Prediction-Final-Report-1dy57cu.docx

Schuck, P. (1984). The transformation of immigration law. *Columbia Law Review, 84*(1), 1–90.

Schuck, P. (2018). *Citizens, strangers, and in-betweens: Essays on immigration and citizenship.* New York, NY: Routledge.

Seggie, F. N., & Sanford, G. (2010). Perceptions of female Muslim students who veil: Campus religious climate. *Race Ethnicity and Education, 13*(1), 59–82.

Southern Poverty Law Center. (2016a). *Ten days after: Harassment and intimidation in the aftermath of the election.* Retrieved from https://www.splcenter.org/sites/default/files/com_hate_incidents_report_2017_update.pdf

Southern Poverty Law Center. (2016b). *Update: 1,094 bias-related incidents in the month following the election.* Retrieved from https://www.splcenter.org/hatewatch/2016/12/16/update-1094-bias-related-incidents-month-following-election

Southern Poverty Law Center. (2017). *Frequency of noose hate crimes incidents surge.* Retrieved from https://www.splcenter.org/hatewatch/2017/06/05/frequency-noose-hate-crime-incidents-surges

USA PATRIOT Act: Preserving life and liberty: Uniting and strengthening America by providing appropriate tools required to intercept and obstruct terrorism, Pub. L. No. 107-56, 115 Stat. 272 (2001). https://www.justice.gov/archive/ll/highlights.htm

U.S. Const. amend. XIV.

Will, M. (2015, March 11). Across North Carolina, Muslim students take stock of a trying semester. *The Chronicle of Higher Education.* Retrieved from http://www.chronicle.com/article/Across-North-Carolina-Muslim/228327

5

QUEER MUSLIMS

Shafiqa Ahmadi and Sama Shah

Queer Muslims live in the margins of both queer and Muslim communities, two communities that are in the margins of a larger society plagued with homophobia and Islamophobia that legitimize injustices in society and promote religious, racial, and gender discrimination (Ahmadi, 2012; Crenshaw, 1989). Thus, discussion solely focused on only religion, only gender, or only sexuality fails to accurately capture the experience of queer Muslims (Crenshaw, 1989). The tendency to treat religion and sexual orientation as mutually exclusive categories of experience and analysis distorts the experiences of queer Muslims and erases them from the discussions of religious and queer discrimination (Ahmadi, 2012). From Gayatri Chakravorty Spivak's (1988) gendered analysis of the effects of colonialism on the subaltern to the work of Black feminists such as bell hooks (1981), Kimberly Crenshaw (1989), and Angela Davis (1983), intersectionality has and continues to be an important lens through which we understand the experiences of those at the crossroads of various oppressions. We must understand that the intersection of multiple systems of oppression creates and shapes one's lived experiences, perceptions, and worldviews, which is critical to comprehension of queer Muslims. In an effort to better understand the experiences of queer Muslims in the United States this chapter will (a) discuss general Muslim experience in postsecondary institutions, (b) explore queer experience in college, and (c) use intersectionality to better understand the specific experiences and needs of queer Muslim college students. This chapter will end with a discussion of implications and recommendations for institutions of higher education as well as questions for class discussion.

Muslim Experiences

To better understand the experiences of Muslim university students, we must look at the effects of 9/11 on the nation's psyche, how it radically changed many Americans' perception of Muslims and immigrants from Muslim-majority nations. Muslims in America, with the exception of converts to Islam and of Black Muslims who are the descendants of enslaved Africans forcibly brought to the United States many generations ago, largely live in a state of diaspora. Not fully of this country nor their homelands, they transcend borders, often shouldering the legacies of colonialism and invasion by Europe and America that left their countries of origin grappling with the past while also coming to terms with their place in this "Western world" (Tindongan, 2011). Based on this idea of Muslims as a diaspora group, in "Negotiating Muslim Youth Identity in a Post-9/11 World," Cynthia White Tindongan (2011) explores Muslim experiences in U.S. public schools through the lens of Edward Said's *Orientalism*, noting that because many Americans have little knowledge of the colonization, occupation, and exploitation of the "Islamic world," they often construct orientalist images of what they perceive as the mainstream Muslim man—hypermasculine, misogynistic, dangerous—and Muslim woman—submissive, oppressed, asexual—thus furthering the othering of Muslims. When we rid ourselves of these orientalist notions, we can begin to understand Muslims in America as constantly negotiating their identities, questioning where they belong, and feeling the pressure to simultaneously defy the negative stereotypes and live up to the myth of Muslims (specifically wealthier Asian and Arab Muslims) as the assimilated doctors, lawyers, and engineers who contribute positively to society, not the terrorists who "hate us"—in essence, being portrayed as a model minority. And still, even if those outside the in-group grow to recognize the complexities of Muslim American identity, Tindongan explains that within the in-group, stereotypes and hierarchies are perpetuated. Using W.E.B. Du Bois's idea of *double consciousness*—when one's perception of self is colored by membership in a marginalized group—Tindongan explains that many Muslims feel the need to shed their Muslim identity in favor of a Western—American—identity, in part because there are hierarchies created in the Muslim community, wherein children of immigrants are seen as whitewashed and more recent immigrants are *boaters* (i.e., refugees who arrive on boats) or *fobs* (i.e., "fresh off the boat"), making the group a difficult space to navigate for many seeking both acceptance outside as well as within the community (Tindongan, 2011). Combined with the pressures of life at university, navigating the various communities that Muslim Americans find themselves a part of proves particularly challenging.

Looking specifically at Muslim women's experiences in the university environment, in "Not Too 'College-Like,' Not Too Normal: American Muslim Undergraduate Women's Gendered Discourses," Shabana Mir (2009) explores the pressure on Muslim women to be both "normal" (i.e., assimilated into mainstream American society) and religious. The perfect balance of the two means that they may be accepted in the Muslim community as well as the non-Muslim/secular university community. Mir highlights that, often, it is women who face the brunt of the burden in preserving the "image" of the faith by not being sexual, flirtatious, too "Western," or otherwise socially liberal. Mir divulges the unique challenges Muslim women face within Muslim communities at U.S. universities, where they may not face scrutiny from their parents but undergo a different kind of judgment from their peers. The case, then, of queer Muslim women is especially complicated as women, they are expected to not engage in sexual or promiscuous behavior, yet, as queer individuals, they are oversexualized, portrayed as sexual deviants, and assumed to have experimented sexually with those of the same gender as an explanation to how they discovered their queerness.

Viewing this pressure on Muslim women, and Muslims at large, to balance their Muslim identity with their American/Western one through the lens of Mahmood Mamdani's (2005) *Good Muslim, Bad Muslim: America, the Cold War, and the Roots of Terror*, we can understand how, within the Muslim community, Western colonial tactics and dichotomies are reinforced. By tracing the roots of Islamism and Islamist violence to the Central Intelligence Agency's involvement in the Soviet-Afghan War, looking specifically at how Islamic rhetoric was manipulated to radicalize Afghan men, Mamdani explores the dichotomy the West sets of "good Muslims" and "bad Muslims"—how, essentially, Muslims must prove their loyalty to the West, how grateful they are to be in the Western countries they reside in, and how committed they are to Western democracy and values in order to attain the good Muslim label. Those speaking against—bad Muslims— are the terrorists, those who hate "us," who are antimodernity and antiliberal (Mamdani, 2005). These strict categories Muslims are boxed into, Mamdani argues, mean that Muslims are, in Western eyes, destined to be either the subservient liberal or the raging extremist. If we try to apply this thinking to Muslim communities in the West, we see that some Muslims adopt these orientalist ways of thinking and, to a certain degree, participate in their own essentialization and categorization of good Muslim and bad Muslim. Going back to Mir's work, a bad Muslim then becomes one who drinks; is sexually active; and, for women specifically, one who does not don the hijab or is perceived as immodest. It can also mean a Muslim who is too radical—if so much focus is centered on balancing being just religious enough and just assimilated enough, a bad Muslim is one who damages the faith by expressing extremist views, either violent ones or ones that run counter to certain "American values" that "mainstream Muslims" (this phrase itself is problematic) have accepted, such as Western democracy and capitalism. Being queer and Muslim can automatically put one in this bad Muslim category, thus furthering this orientalist construct both within a community where homophobia is an issue and outside the community where Islamophobia and homophobia are issues.

Queer Students' College Experience

When looking at queer students' experience in college, we see a similar struggle to fit into a mainstream that is not accepting of queer identities. In her research on academic environments and gender, Jo Freeman (1979) explains that "null environments" (p. 221), ones that are neutral, meaning they do not express support for either gender, were similar to hostile environments because they failed to balance the minimal levels of occupational encouragement women receive. Applying this to college environments and LGBTQ+ students, we can understand open environments to be ones in which dialogue around sexual orientation, gender, and race are encouraged whereas hostile ones are ones in which negative attitudes and comments regarding homosexuality are allowed to exist (Stevens, 2004). Null environments do not exhibit either positive or negative characteristics but have the effect of hostile environments on queer students in many ways (Stevens, 2004). This illustrates that even environments that do not show an openly negative atmosphere toward LGBTQ+ students can feel unwelcoming because the stigma that surrounds being queer makes it important that spaces actively include these individuals so that the taboo can be overcome. Lopez and Chism (1993) shed light on the issue of gay men and lesbian women in classrooms, finding that "demeaning comments about gay and lesbian students [were] especially harmful" (p. 98) whereas comments that illustrated support for LGBTQ+ issues were helpful. Moreover, the study found that professors who self-identified as gay or lesbian fostered a more receptive and safer environment for students (Lopez & Chism, 1993). These studies illustrate the importance of students with nonnormative sexual orientations being in actively supportive environments, where discussion on LGBTQ+ issues is encouraged and where instructors demonstrate support for queer individuals and are able to create an environment of trust.

In a study by Stevens (2004), 11 self-identified gay university men were asked a variety of questions related to "gay identity development consisting of one central category (finding empowerment) and five integrative categories: (a) self-acceptance; (b) disclosure to others; (c) individual factors; (d) environmental influences; and (e) multiple identities exploration" (p. 191). The first category, self-acceptance, involves a "coming out to self," an internal acknowledgment of one's attraction to other men and of "being different" (Stevens, 2004, p. 191). Overall, much of this stage involves the individual recognizing and accepting his gay identity. It is a difficult stage, and often forces the individual to unlearn many of the negative stereotypes and preconceptions of what homosexuality means and looks like—in essence, a form of internalized homophobia (Stevens, 2004). There are similarities between the queer community and Muslim community in struggles regarding identifying with a community and a fear of being stereotyped based on people's notions of what the most visible members of the community look or act like. For the Muslim community, this leads to internalized Islamophobia, and for the queer community, internalized homophobia. One can imagine that queer Muslims, at the intersections of these two oppressions, have to manage great levels of internalized prejudice, adding to psychological stress and struggles of self-acceptance.

The second category, disclosure to others, can be understood as the popular "coming out" (Stevens, 2004, p. 193) event in which there is some sort of verbal acknowledgment to parents, siblings, friends, or others of one's gay identity. Entering this stage requires great courage from participants, and participants reported that even though their family members existed outside the university setting they played a great role in their lives at university (Stevens, 2004). Disclosure also opened the channels to the creation of a strong support network that these men would rely on in the future (Stevens, 2004). Support networks were crucial in developing a sense of empowerment in queer men, leading to an increase in confidence and self-assurance, whereas personally held negative stereotypes of participants led to attitudes that marginalized other gay men within the community (Stevens, 2004). For example, effeminate gay men often found themselves ostracized in the gay community because more masculine gay men did not want to be associated with the "effeminate stereotype" (Stevens, 2004, p. 192). Moreover, religious groups were stereotyped as "homophobic and self-righteous" (p. 195), which is isolating for gay men who also identify as religious in general and Muslim specifically (Stevens, 2004, p. 192). Furthermore, men of color expressed a fear of rejection in a community that seemed to place greater value on Whiteness.

In the third category, many individual factors combine to create a unique experience for each individual gay man, and the narrative is clearly complicated when intersecting identities that are oppressed come into play. However, environmental influences, those outside an individual's perceptions and fears, also contribute to feelings of comfort in one's sexuality on college campuses (Stevens, 2004). In this study, environmental influences, the fourth category, were described as relationships; locations; signs, symbols, and resources; discrimination; and stereotypes (Stevens, 2004). Relationships included an individual's friends and family members as well as other people the individual deemed as holding positions of power or influence in their lives, such as a professor (Stevens, 2004). Environment also had an influence on how included students feel on campus; safe space stickers indicated staff, faculty, and students in the office who were open, motivated, and accepting of queer identities (Stevens, 2004). The environment created in the university as well as the actions and words of professors and other administrators has an important effect on queer individuals, meaning there is room for growth in this area. The last category was reached when these individuals felt comfortable enough in their queer identity to then explore how this identity intersects with their other identities to shape their experiences—for example, how being queer as well as a student of color shapes their sense of belonging within both the queer community and another marginalized community (Stevens, 2004).

In a survey of queer students at 25 small liberal arts colleges in the United States, Bridget Harr and Emily Kane (2008) set out to determine how supportive queer students are of an intersectional approach to queer politics, looking specifically at attitudes toward inclusivity and coalition building. This study concluded that most queer students were supportive of highlighting issues of race, with 78% of respondents indicating their preference for some or a great deal of attention to be paid to race (Harr & Kane, 2008). Rahman (2010) and data collected by the Al-Fatiha Foundation indicate that there is an overrepresentation of White queers in the LGBTQ+ community. However, queer students from less privileged backgrounds (in terms of race, class, gender identification, sexuality identification) were more likely than queer students from more privileged backgrounds to use *queer politics*, meaning that "colleges with a greater presence of less-privileged or marginalized students were more likely to have queer student organizations that utilized queer politics" (Harr & Kane, 2008,

p. 296). These data not only illustrate queer students' engagement with issues of race but also demonstrate the need for sexual orientation–focused groups to highlight the voices of those who are less privileged—LGBTQ+ Muslims fit into the category given their lack of representation in queer spaces.

Intersection of Oppression

According to Momin Rahman, queer Muslims complicate two narratives. First, queerness is a Western concept in opposition to the "Eastern" religion of Islam and its understanding of masculinity, thus challenging the category of Muslim. Second, queer Muslims, through their expressions of faith, particularly a faith commonly viewed as inherently hostile toward the LGBTQ+ community, challenge the category of queer (Rahman, 2010). Thus, in order for queer Muslims to truly experience liberation, notions of both what it means to be Muslim and what it means to be queer must be "problematized and challenged" (Rahman, 2010, p. 950) to include those at the intersections—LGBTQ+ Muslims—who are affected by converging oppressions. Thus, when multiple systems of oppression such as racism, Islamophobia, and homophobia intersect, the intersection shapes the lived experiences of LGBTQ+ Muslims. It is the imposition of one burden on another burden that creates intersectional oppression and subordination.

In line with Rahman's ideas that intersectionality is crucial to understanding the lived experiences of queer Muslims, the Al-Fatiha Foundation, which began a process of legal dissolution in 2011 after its founder, Pakistani American Faisal Alam, stepped down, was an organization dedicated to advocating for the rights of LGBTQ+ Muslims. The foundation conducted in-depth interviews with queer Muslims, and a selection of these interviews about queer Muslims' relationships with both their sexual orientation and faith was published in the journal *Culture, Health and Sexuality* (see Minwalla, Rosser, Feldman, & Varga, 2005). What emerged from these interviews was a complex narrative of how queer Muslims balance community pressures, sexual desires, faith, Islamophobia, and homophobia all at once—with some turning away from religion completely, others being drawn closer, and still others whose relationship with faith cannot be boiled down to a single descriptor. For many queer Muslims, the prevailing view that homosexuality is a sin in Islam served as an alienating force that pushed them toward shame and seclusion. Many felt that it was not permissible to be both queer and Muslim, which created an internal and external sense of conflict

(Minwalla, Rosser, Feldman, & Varga, 2005). Yet for others, religion became an escape from marriage pressures and other community and family expectations (Minwalla et al., 2005). Both examples illustrate reconciling sexual orientation with religious doctrine and community pressures that are difficult for many queer Muslims. This pressure, combined with personal struggle and alienation from the larger Muslim community, often complicates queer Muslims' relationships with faith, perhaps indicating that traditional faith-based organizations as well as non-faith-based organizations need to challenge their understanding of the "Muslim experience."

Younes Mourchid (2010), in "The Dialectics of Islamophobia and Homophobia in the Lives of Gay Muslims in the United States," further explores the narratives of Muslims who experienced such profound alienation that they renounced faith altogether, with some veering into Islamophobia as a result of deep emotional pain. Although controversial, one can argue that these beliefs stem not from an irrational hatred of Islam, but rather a profound sense of hurt that is associated with a supposedly intolerant religion as opposed to homophobic individuals. For some, distinguishing between homophobia and Islamic doctrine has proved difficult, resulting in internalization of Islamophobia due to the intense homophobic attitudes of some within the Muslim community.

However, not all gay Muslims internalize Islamophobia or renounce their faith despite facing similar aggressions from some heterosexual Muslims, thus complicating the image of the LGBTQ+ community as entirely nonreligious. In fact, many queer Muslims have taken the story of Lut, traditionally thought to be a condemnation of homosexuality, and through their understanding of Islam have interpreted it to be a condemnation of rape and violence in war as a tool of shaming, not a condemnation of same-sex relationships.

In this way, many queer Muslims reconcile their sexuality and faith by reading the portions of the Qur'an and the parts of the Sunnah—the sayings and deeds of the Prophet Muhammad—that highlight how traditional Islamic ideals of justice should apply to sexual orientations or those who express gender outside the traditional binary. These Muslim students take interpretation into their own hands, looking for meaning and understanding beyond the traditional viewpoints (Minwalla et al., 2005). Likewise, not all queer Muslims cope with stigma by distancing themselves from other Muslims; rather, they seek out Muslims from similar ethnic backgrounds as a way to build supportive social circles. In the study of queer Muslim men conducted by the Al-Fatiha Foundation, this tendency for gay Muslims to seek out those from similar ethnic and faith backgrounds is, for some, motivated by the fact that many Muslim queers of color grew up seeing only White queerness represented in the media. Seeing whiteness as attractive and the predominant representation of queerness as White individuals, reinforced through movies, TV, and magazines, socialized many queer Muslims to believe that there were no queer Muslims. As a result of growing up with few images of queers of color and of Islamic faith, many gay Muslims spend the majority of their youth and teenage years struggling with internalized racism, only beginning to appreciate their heritage later in life and, in some cases, looking for partners who share similar backgrounds as both gay and Muslim. There is a comfort level and affirmation in dating someone from your own background, someone who understands cultural, religious, and traditional norms and the complexities that queer Muslims face and fight to belong to and be accepted in.

Discussion and Recommendations

There is no one way to be a queer Muslim—for some, their sexual orientation draws them closer to faith; for others, it pushes them to apostasy; and still for others, it takes them on a long, and often lifetime, struggle of reconciliation between religious scripture and identity. Either way, no one LGBTQ+ Muslim is like the next, and each has unique needs based on their specific sexual identity as well as other intersecting identities such as race, class, gender, and national origin. What can be agreed on, as Mourchid (2010) elaborates, is that, irrespective of interpretations of the Qur'an and Sunnah, "the educational system can bridge the divide between two different views," resulting in a dialogue "not about who is right or wrong . . . but about the presentation of objective facts, diversity of perspectives, and, above all, about tolerance and respect of the differing points of view" (p. 200). Unfortunately, there is not much literature available regarding the experiences of queer Muslims and of queer Muslim university students in particular, making it difficult for educators and institutions to empathize with the uniqueness of the queer Muslim experience and come to a deeper understanding of the effects of homophobia and Islamophobia when they intersect and oppress LGBTQ+ Muslims.

In "Reconsidering Campus Diversity: An Examination of Muslim Students' Experiences," Shafiqa Ahmadi and Darnell Cole (2010) examine how rising national interest in Islam post-9/11 has affected the experiences of Muslim university students, and how the Muslim student experience differs from the Christian or Jewish student experience. In contrast to Christian and Jewish university students, Muslim students "spent more time attending racial/cultural awareness workshops, having a roommate of a different race/

ethnicity, [and] socializing with someone of a different racial/ethnic group" (p. 135). In addition to engaging in more frequent interactions with diverse student groups, "Muslim students also indicated that they spent more time working on group projects in class and in religious service, prayer, and meditation than Jewish students" (p. 134). However, given that this study does not break down the category of Muslim into subcategories such as Muslim women or Muslim men, or, in our case, heterosexual Muslims and LGBTQ+ Muslims, we cannot be sure if queer Muslims experience the same level of interaction with diverse student demographics or if they spend an equal amount of time partaking in religious services as other Muslims, or even as members of other faith groups, given the homophobia present in many communities of faith. Studying the marginalized within marginalized groups, comparing the college experiences of queer Muslims to the experiences of queer Christian or Jewish students, would increase the scope and depth of knowledge about Muslim students. Research that focuses on better understanding specific resources that queer Muslim students might need to feel welcome both in campus faith organizations and in the university at large is essential.

As Ahmadi and Cole (2010) argue, further research is needed to understand why Muslim college students feel less satisfied with their educational experiences than students from other faith backgrounds (particularly Jewish students); narrowing down the topic to focus on queer Muslims is important to understanding campus diversity as a whole. Research on LGBTQ+ Muslims and how their intersecting identities and oppressions affect their satisfaction and well-being ultimately allows administrators and institutions to craft campus diversity initiatives around an appreciation for the multifaceted ways in which an individual can be Muslim and express "Muslimness." Studying the experiences of LGBTQ+ Muslim students can lead to better programming and outreach efforts for all Muslim students across college campuses. In this way, we can understand that just as Muslim Student Associations (MSAs) can work with universities to unpack prior assumptions about Muslims, so can LGBTQ+ groups on college campuses, from queer and ally student associations to more specialized professional organizations for queer students, challenge their notion of what a queer individual looks like and what religion they may practice.

There is a clear gap in the discourse surrounding the experiences of Muslim university students and queer Muslims, resulting in an even deeper lack of knowledge about the experiences of queer Muslim university students. For campus administrators whose job it is to promote diversity and combat institutional prejudice, as well as for MSAs and LGBTQ+ student organizations, understanding the unique experiences of these students at the intersections is critical to ensuring all students receive equitable treatment within the university campus. Addressing Islamophobia, homophobia, and the intersection of multiple burdens of oppressions can help combat discrimination in higher education and create understanding among diverse students, faculty, and staff.

Discussion Questions

1. To what extent are queer Muslim students' experiences similar to or different from their peers'?
2. On a college campus, who should be responsible for addressing issues of race, ethnicity, and religion as they relate to the experiences of queer Muslim students?
3. To what extent do you believe Muslim student organizations and/or queer student organizations should address issues pertaining to queer Muslim students?

References

Ahmadi, S. (2012). Islam and homosexuality: Religious dogma, colonial rule, and the quest for belonging. *Journal of Civil Rights and Economic Development, 26*(3), art. 2.

Ahmadi, S., & Cole, D. (2010). Reconsidering campus diversity: An examination of Muslim students' experiences. *The Journal of Higher Education, 81*(2), 121–139.

Crenshaw, K. (1989). Demarginalizing the intersection of race and sex: A black feminist critique of antidiscrimination doctrine, feminist theory and antiracist politics. *University of Chicago Legal Forum*, 1989(1);139–167

Davis, A. Y. (1983). *Women, race & class.* New York: Vintage Books.

Freeman, J. (1979). How to discriminate against women without really trying. In J. Freeman (Ed.), *Women: A feminist perspective* (2nd ed., pp. 217–232). Palo Alto, CA: Mayfield.

Harr, B. E., & Kane, E. W. (2008). Intersectionality and queer student support for queer politics. *Race, Gender & Class, 15*(3/4), 283–299.

hooks, bell. (1981). *Ain't I a woman: Black women and feminism* (1st ed.). South End Press.

Lopez, G., & Chism, N. (1993). Classroom concerns of gay and lesbian students: The invisible minority. *College Teaching, 41*(3), 97–103.

Mamdani, M. (2005). *Good Muslim, bad Muslim: America, the Cold War, and the roots of terror.* New York, NY: Three Leaves Press.

Minwalla, O., Rosser, S. B. R., Feldman, J., & Varga, C. (2005). Identity experience among progressive gay Muslims in North America: A qualitative study within Al-Fatiha. *Culture, Health & Sexuality, 7*(2), 113–128.

Mir, S. (2009). Not too "college-like," not too normal: American Muslim undergraduate women's gendered discourses. *Anthropology & Education Quarterly, 40*(3), 237–256.

Mourchid, Y. (2010). The dialectics of Islamophobia and homophobia in the lives of gay Muslims in the United States. *Counterpoints, 346,* 187–203.

Rahman, M. (2010). Queer as intersectionality: Theorizing gay Muslim identities. *Sociology, 44*(5), 944–961.

Spivak, Gayatri C. (1988). Can the Subaltern Speak? In Cary Nelson and Lawrence Grossberg (Eds.), *Marxism and the Interpretation of Culture.* Champaign, IL: University of Illinois Press.

Stevens, R. A. (2004). Understanding gay identity development within the college environment. *Journal of College Student Development, 45*(2), 185–206.

Tindongan, C. W. (2011). Negotiating Muslim youth identity in a post-9/11 world. *High School Journal, 95*(1), 72–87.

6

BLACK MUSLIMS

Darnell Cole, Liane Hypolite, and Alex Atashi

On January 7, 2019, *The Hill* published an article titled "Muslim, Black Congresswomen Pose for Photo Together: 'Representation Matters.'" The piece was inspired by a picture that was tweeted depicting Ayanna Pressley of Massachusetts and Ilhan Omar of Minnesota, who posted the tweet, ending with the caption "Representation matters." The article about this post goes on to state, "Omar is one of the first two Muslim women elected to Congress, and Pressley is the first black woman elected to Congress from Massachusetts" (Anapol, 2019, para. 2). The article describes Omar as the "first Somali-American member of Congress, [who] will be the first person to wear a hijab on the House floor after being granted a religious exemption to a 181-year-old rule banning hats on the chamber floor" (Anapol, 2019, para. 4). Although this article accurately describes important identities that both Pressley and Omar embrace, it also illustrates that in the American imagination there is an overemphasis not on the policies or public issues Omar represents but on her (a) religious identity as a Muslim woman; (b) her article of clothing, hijab, that she chooses to wear on and off the House floor; and (c) her national origin and immigrant status as a Somali refugee.

Interestingly, even within the racialized American context, Omar's racial identity as a Black woman is erased. In contrast, there is a specific focus on Pressley's racial identity, and her religious identity is not mentioned. Such a critical omission is yet another example of the separation of Black and Muslim identities as evidenced throughout American history. This manner of labeling serves as a mechanism to further divide and conquer systemically marginalized populations, pitting one group against the other. Such strategies echo what scholars like Ange-Marie Hancock (2011) term *oppression Olympics*, where debates about inequality devolve into competitions about who holds the most oppressed positions. Many scholars have asserted, as a counterargument, that the path to justice requires an intersectional perspective, where understanding how systems of power and privilege manifest in the lives of those whose identities are not isolated like discrete items on a list, but instead reflect dynamic daily experiences where one's social identities are intertwined (Cho, Crenshaw, & McCall, 2013; Crenshaw, 1991; Hancock, 2011). Black Muslims experience forced divisions of their worlds that, in reality, overlap and converge. Unfortunately, Black Muslim students in the college context must also contend with this dilemma, which has real implications for how they navigate their college experiences, as well as the campus policies and practices that influence their everyday lives.

The complexity of the Black Muslim identity is also challenged and misunderstood within Black and Muslim communities. In the American context today, Black communities are most often associated with the Christian church, and more affiliated explicitly with Protestants in the Baptist denomination, in terms of the dominant religious identity (Sahgal & Smith, 2009). A 2014 Pew Research Center study of over 35,000 survey respondents across the United States determined that 79% identified as being Christian, where over half of those individuals identified as historically Black Protestant in particular, compared to only 2% of the respondents identifying as Muslim. Additionally, African Americans generally report being more religious than the U.S. population overall, showing higher levels of religious service attendance and average frequency of prayer (Sahgal & Smith, 2009). This context offers a critical backdrop for understanding the religious tensions within the Black American demographic, particularly given the overall homogeneity of their Christian-based religious affiliations. This broader context can be at odds with distinct pockets of Black Muslims who can be minoritized by the general U.S. population as well as within a Black Christian intraracial majority.

When considering the overall Muslim population in the United States, Black Muslims are estimated to account for 20% of the Muslim population (Mohamed & Diamant, 2019). Furthermore, about half of the Black Muslim community in the United States are converts to Islam (Mohamed & Diamant, 2019). Despite their clear presence as Muslims, Black Muslims are often not represented in the media. Typically, images of Muslims in the United States are of Arab and South Asian immigrants (Green, 2017). The lack of representation in the American media contributes to the minoritization of Black Muslims, who are often discriminated against because of both their race and their religion. Even within Muslim communities, Black Muslims face racism. Muslim leader Hamza Yusuf, who cofounded the Muslim liberal arts college Zaytuna College, recently demonstrated anti-Blackness in the Muslim community at a conference in December 2016. When asked about Black Lives Matter, he responded that the United States is "one of the least racist societies in the world" and that of the homicides in the United States "fifty percent are black-on-black crime, literally" (Green, 2017, para. 2). He later stated that "the biggest crisis facing the African American community in the United States is not racism. It is the breakdown of the black family" (Green, 2017, para. 2). Both of his racist comments faced massive and justified backlash from Muslims who were disturbed by his anti-Blackness (para. 10). These comments, which came from someone who many see as an American Muslim leader, are just one type of racism Black Muslims experience at the intersection of their social identities. Many Black Muslims note the everyday racism they experience in their lives from fellow Muslims of Arab or Southeast Asian descent (Green, 2017). Black Muslims face discrimination not only by Americans outside of the Muslim community because of their race and religion but also within their Muslim community because they are Black.

To further explore this underresearched topic, this chapter begins with the little known historical context of Black Muslims and, for some, their forced enslavement during a significant period in the early development of the United States. The following section explores the more recent context for laws, policies, and politics that have shaped Islamophobia and the subsequent marginality of Black Muslims. We then focus on institutions of higher education, not only outlining how Muslim and Black students have been understood by existing literature but also offering how students who share this dynamic identity face unique challenges in college settings. Finally, we provide recommendations for practitioners to suggest how postsecondary systems can better support the needs of Black Muslim students in ways that recognize their unique histories, contexts, and experiences.

A Brief Historical Context of Black Muslim Americans

Through a collection of historical documents, scholars are developing a more nuanced and better understanding of how Muslims who also identify as Black, African, or African American have had a significant influence on the United States (Austin, 2012; Curtis, 2012; Khabeer, 2016; Lincoln, 1994; Mamiya, 1982). Within the context of these historical analyses are critical sociopolitical and socioeconomic movements from Black liberation to civil rights to the ongoing reconstruction of Black religious identity, which includes "Black Muslims"—a specific reference to a term attributed to Lincoln (1961) about "the Lost-Found Nation Islam . . . established by Master Wali

Farrad Muhammad, alias Wallace Fard, in Detroit in 1930" (Mamiya, 1982, p. 138). More recent is Khabeer's (2016) *Muslim Cool*, which documents an ethnographic movement that offers an insightful sociocultural analysis and ethnoreligious critique "at the intersection of Islam and hip hop" (p. 2). The term *Muslim cool*, as defined by Khabeer (2016), "is a way of being Muslim that draws on Blackness to contest two overlapping systems of racial norms: the hegemonic ethnoreligious norms of Arab and South Asian U.S. American Muslim communities on the one hand, and White American normativity on the other" (p. 2). Within the context of this chapter, however, Black Muslim references Muslims whose racial and ethnic identity is Black, African, or African American.

As early as 1501, when the first Africans were enslaved and forced into ships traveling to regions of the New World, the religion of Islam had already expanded across many African nations by way of trade, the conversion of rulers, and religious wars and invasions (Diouf, 1998). Followers of the Islamic faith grew and influenced local African cultures and traditions. They remained a minority in the broader population, though nonetheless a significant part of the West African region. It was primarily in these areas where people were enslaved and brought by force to the Caribbean and the Americas, including the American colonies (Diouf, 1998). Therefore, it is estimated that 15% to 30% of the enslaved Black African population brought to the United States when slavery began in the early 1600s were Muslim (Muhammad, 2013).

Even though they were categorized as Black slaves, some Black Muslims tried to maintain their Islamic religious identity by holding on to their religious holidays, traditions, and daily rituals even as they were banned due to the numerous restrictions and mandates put in place by slave codes (Beydoun, 2014; Diouf, 1998). Slave codes made religious activity a crime in the American South (Beydoun, 2014). Despite efforts to convert and quiet their Islamic identities, some enslaved African Muslims drew from religious teachings, literacy, and language to build a resistance. Letters and diaries help explain how they used Arabic to communicate strategically about verses from the Qur'an, genealogical lists, and their desires to return to Africa—all under the radar of slave owners (Amon, 2017). Others survived by taking part in pseudo-Christian conversions (Amon, 2017). In a similar effort to further separate them from their homes, histories, and identities, enslaved people were forced to take the often Christian names given to them by their owners (Diouf, 1998).

As Beydoun (2014) argues, this history is limited given the intentional separation of Black and Muslim identities enforced by U.S. law and slaveholders at the time, which has led to a limited historical understanding of this population. Additionally, as Diouf (1998) contends, the enslavement of people throughout history was not new, but "what became unique was that by the sixteenth century Europeans reserved slavery for the Africans" (p. 16). It is this particular cross section of associating the social construction of a Black racial identity with slavery happening in conjunction with the erasure of non-Christian religious practices that allowed for the historical disappearance of the collective Black Muslim American identity.

Laws, Policies, and Politics

Since the foundation of the United States, Black Muslim Americans have been stripped of their identities and controlled by White supremacy, laws, and policies. Black Americans, which includes both Christian and Muslim leaders such as Martin Luther King Jr. and Malcolm X, have had to fight for basic civil rights since slavery, and continue to face racism and denial of those civil rights today. In the media, through harassment and hate crimes, and in governmental policy, Muslim Americans have been and continue to be treated negatively, and certainly different from other religious groups. Black Muslim Americans have had to face the compounding intersection of their identities since slavery, and continue to be controlled by present-day laws and policies like the Countering Violent Extremism Taskforce and the program around Black Identity Extremism.

The concept of countering violent extremism (CVE) has been ingrained in the national security strategies and political landscape of the United States for years (Patel & Koushik, 2017). However, it became a central part of counterterrorism policy in 2011 when President Barack Obama laid out the National Strategy for Empowering Local Partners to Prevent Violent Extremism in the United States (Executive Office of the President of the United States, 2011a), as well as the follow-up implementation plan (Executive Office of the President of the United States, 2011b). The term *countering violent extremism* in itself appears to be broad in its purpose and scope. However, the aim is specifically at Muslim communities in practice (Patel & Koushik, 2017). The introduction to the both documents specifically name al-Qa'ida's "violent ideology" as the root of the problem they are attempting to address in the United States. The al-Qa'ida organization has declared itself as a representative of true Islam, which has caused the entire Muslim community to be blamed and feared for their actions; that representation, however, is inaccurate (Helfstein, Abdullah, & al-Obaidi, 2009). In a study done by the Countering Terrorism Center at West Point on al-Qa'ida's violence against Muslims, it was found that a vast majority of victims of al-Qa'ida's terrorism were Muslims (Helfstein et al., 2009). Because al-Qa'ida's hateful ideology is falsely associated with Islam, the focus of the strategy report and implementation plan is placed directly on Muslim communities. Creating new policies by politicizing the fear of terrorism is not unique in being used to justify control over Muslim communities. The USA PATRIOT Act, following September 11, 2001, had a similar impact (Ahmadi, 2011).

Although the strategy report and implementation plan were presented as positive, community-based interventions, they directed law enforcement to use targeted tactics toward Muslim communities, like surveillance, prosecutions, and investigations, with no empirical support or justification (Executive Office of the President of the United States, 2011a, 2011b; Patel & Koushik, 2017). By creating an environment of suspicion based on subjective measures, CVE fails Muslim Americans and presents them as threatening (Zogby, 2015). In doing so, CVE makes Muslim Americans susceptible to discrimination and dangerous treatment from law enforcement and the broader community in which they reside. Although non-Muslims committed almost all (94%) of the terrorist attacks in the United States during 1980–2005, the Trump administration has discussed taking its control on Muslims a step further, by potentially renaming the CVE program to "Countering Islamic Extremism" or "Countering Radical Islamic Extremism," while also implementing travel bans on several Muslim-majority countries (Ainsley, Volz, & Cooke, 2017; Federal Bureau of Investigation [FBI], 2005). The federal government's creation of its Countering Violent Extremism Taskforce and the Muslim bans is evidence that Muslims in the United States are viewed as threatening and as potential terrorists that need to be curtailed and controlled.

The federal government continues to demonstrate its viewpoint of Muslims as threatening terrorists with its 2017 FBI report. In August 2017, the FBI Counterterrorism Division wrote an intelligence assessment report titled *Black Identity Extremists Likely Motivated to Target Law Enforcement Officers*, marking the formal creation of the Black Identity Extremists (BIEs) group by the government. The FBI (2017) assessed that "it is very likely Black Identity Extremists' (BIE) perceptions of police brutality against African Americans spurred an increase in premeditated, retaliatory lethal violence against law enforcement and will very likely serve as justification for such violence" (p. 2). The assessment is problematic for many reasons. Notably, it uses language such as "perceptions of police brutality" that refuses to acknowledge the reality of police violence and brutality against people of color. The report then goes on to name six specific incidents since 2014 that they believe are "very likely" to be acts of retaliation for "perceived" police brutality incidents (FBI, 2017, p. 4). The continued use of perception, rather than acknowledging the reality of the conflicts, contradicts their assessment of retaliation. Additionally, the use of *very likely* is defined in the report's appendix as highly probable, with an 80% to 95% chance and likelihood. The report then states another contradiction that "BIE violence has been rare over the past 20 years" (p. 6). It is at best irresponsible, and at worst a provocation, to assess such a high likelihood for BIEs to participate in premeditated violence against law enforcement while also acknowledging BIEs as a historically nonviolent group.

When reading through the FBI report, one important Black activist group is not mentioned. Black Lives Matter, a movement started in 2013 by three Black women and organizers—Alicia Garza, Patrisse Cullors, and Opal Tometi—is not named in the report directly. However, the FBI report mentions specific incidents in recent history that they believed sparked Black Identity Extremism, such as the killing of Michael Brown in Ferguson, Missouri, in 2014 (FBI, 2017). The Black Lives Matter network acknowledges Michael Brown's murder as part of their *herstory* (Black Lives Matter, 2018). Additionally, the rise of Black Lives Matter as a movement and the FBI's assessment of when Black Identity Extremism became a concept are on similar timelines of 2013 and 2014. As soon as activists and protesters of color gain traction and support in their fight against injustices, the government responds and dubs them terrorists (Matthews & Cyril, 2017); this is yet another example of the U.S. government controlling the identities, laws, and policies that impact minoritized people of color.

Black Muslim Americans' identities and existence are compounded by the U.S. government's laws and policies. When examining the policy perspectives of both CVE and Black Identity Extremism, the similarities are striking. Both policies are inspired by a perceived threat from a minoritized group. Both policies use fear to justify their actions, yet are unfounded by statistics. Both policies create a more hostile environment for certain groups of Americans, namely Black and Muslim Americans. By designating both Black and Muslim Americans as terrorists or the "other," the federal government is removing them as part of the American ideal (Ahmadi, 2011). Black Muslim Americans are vulnerable not only because of their religious identity but also because of their racial identity. As they are being surveilled for potential radical terrorism, they are also being monitored for speaking out and acting against racial injustice and police brutality (Beydoun & Hansford, 2017). The intersection of anti-Black and anti-Muslim laws and policies created by the federal government systematically oppresses and controls Black Muslim Americans.

Student Experiences in U.S. Higher Education

Much of the research and empirically grounded scholarship in higher education that focuses on race/ethnicity or religious preference does so in mutually exclusive ways. As a result, the following sections address the literature on Black college students and then Black Muslim college students as a way to contextualize the nature and quality of Black Muslim student experiences among their racial/ethnic peers within higher education.

Black College Students

Higher education literature has increasingly studied the experiences and outcomes for Black college students across institution types, including public (Harper, 2006) and private (Aronson, Fried, & Good, 2002; Robinson-Wood, 2009), two-year (Sandoval-Lucero, Maes, & Klingsmith, 2014; Wood & Harris, 2015) and four-year (Tichavakunda, 2017), as well as predominantly White (Grier-Reed, 2013; Strayhorn, 2014; Williamson, 1999) and historically Black institutions (Brown & Davis, 2001; Byars-Winston, 2006). Studies have ranged from topics such as racial identity formation (Johnson & Arbona, 2006; Sanchez, 2013), peer (Strayhorn, 2008) and faculty (Cole & Griffin, 2013; Lundberg & Schreiner, 2004) interactions, campus service use (Patton, 2006; Strayhorn, Terrell, Redmond, & Walton, 2012), major-specific (Good, Halpin, & Halpin, 2002), and campus climate experiences (Griffin, Cunningham, & George Mwangi, 2016; Solorzano, Ceja, & Yosso, 2000). Although varied in their theoretical approaches, methods, and findings, this body of literature primarily speaks to the diversity of experiences of Black students, who carry many identities. In addition to complex racial and social constructions, these students must manage the nuanced ways that racialized systemic injustices manifest into their day-to-day experiences across higher education institutions.

One facet of Black students' collective identities that remains understudied is their religious and spiritual experiences in college. Some research has pointed to African Americans as having higher rates of religious participation in comparison to the general U.S. population (Christian & Barbarin, 2001; Constantine, Lewis, Conner, & Sanchez, 2000; Constantine, Miville, Warren, Gainor, & Lewis-Coles, 2006). For college students in particular, studies have found positive associative outcomes between Black students and their spirituality or religious affiliations. Studies have found that Black students who reported higher rates of religious participation and spiritual beliefs also tended to report a greater sense of self and connection to their life's purpose (Blaine & Crocker, 1995; Herndon, 2003). Others have drawn associations between religiosity and spirituality to aspects of college life, such as adjustment (Phillips, 2000), coping (Riggins, McNeal, & Herndon, 2008), and academic performance (Walker & Dixon, 2002). For the studies that provide detailed breakdowns of their sample that offer specific religious affiliations, they often consist of mostly Christian participants of various denominations (Blaine & Crocker, 1995; Herndon, 2003; Phillips, 2000). This focus on the exclusion of other religions speaks to a persistent gap in the literature about the specific experiences of Black Muslim college students.

Black Muslim College Students

When looking at the major religious groups globally, Muslims have made exceptional gains in educational achievement in the past three generations (Pew Research Center, 2016). Specifically in North America, the population of Muslims ages 25 and older is 1.8 million, and that population has an average of 13.6 years of schooling (Pew Research Center, 2016). However, there are layers of Islamophobia in media representations, stereotypes, and marginalization that negatively impact the experiences of Muslim college students (Ahmadi, Cole, & Prado, 2018). As the Muslim population is expected to continue to grow and advance in educational achievement, and implications from the Muslim bans remain to be seen in higher education, it is essential to carefully consider the experiences of Muslims in higher education (Ahmadi et al., 2018; Pew Research Center, 2016, 2017a, 2017b).

Although higher education literature exists about the experiences of Muslim students and Black students, there is a gap when considering the experiences and realities of Black Muslim college students. As found by McGuire, Casanova, and Davis (2016), Black Muslims at predominantly White institutions face challenges in finding support and a community. Black Muslim college students are burdened with navigating how their religious and racial identities intersect, leading to further marginalization.

The laws and policies that impact Black Muslims in the United States carry over to affect how Black Muslim college students experience their higher education institutions. When considering present-day policies like CVE and Black Identity Extremism, Black Muslims are considered threatening because of their race and religion. Black Muslim college students who use their free speech and expression on campus are subject to differential treatment compared to their peer students because of these policies.

Recommendations for Higher Education

There are several practical recommendations and policy implications for students, academics, and student affairs practitioners, as well as the senior administrative leadership within postsecondary institutions. For Black Muslim students, knowing *where* and *how* to access, or even establish, the support networks they need, as both a racial and religious minority on campus, can have a tremendous influence on their college engagement and overall educational experience. As such, student affairs practitioners have to be creative in making transparent opportunities at the intersection of Black Muslim students' racial and religious identities. For instance, programming events and activities that foster and encourage authentic collaboration between Black cultural centers and religious life could pose relatively straightforward opportunities that Black Christian students have long been able to take advantage of—typically through gospel choir performances during Black History Month and cosponsored Easter holiday events. Collaborations during Eid al-Fitr and Black History Month may likely prompt similar opportunities for cocurricular programming that functions within the intersection of Black Muslim students.

Administrators in academic affairs have to be prepared to help both students and faculty navigate academic and curricular experiences so that Black Muslim students' experiences are not muted, ignored, or overgeneralized because they occupy marginalized racial and religious identities. Practitioners, perhaps, are in the best position to strategically support the intersection of Black Muslim students' identities. In particular, academic and student affairs practitioners have a specific set of responsibilities to not only assist these students but also create the conditions where non-Muslim and non–Black Muslim students understand, learn about, and meaningfully interact with Black Muslim students. The curricular and classroom experience, as well as cocurricular experiences, must facilitate interracial, intraracial, and interreligious interactions, as well as share complex and nuanced information about critical forms of intersectional social identities—mainly when students are demographically represented within the campus milieu and the local community. Practitioners should establish and facilitate thoughtful coalitions between student organizations; target relevant sociopolitical moments to leverage interactions between student organizations and academic units; and institutionalize signature programs and interventions that incentivize students, cultural/religious support centers, and academic departments.

Academic and student affairs practitioners influence the extent to which Black Muslim students experience Islamophobia on campus, and the institutions' academic leadership can have a tremendous impact on deinstitutionalizing Islamophobia as well. For instance, when the state of Hawaii filed a court case against the Trump administration's Muslim ban, Hawaii

> argued that the travel ban would cause families of Hawaiian residents to be separated, harm the University of Hawaii and do damage to 'the public as a whole inflicted by a radical departure from the status quo that had existed for decades.' (quoted in Higgins, 2018, para. 14)

Additionally, understanding the direct and indirect effect of CVE and Black Identity Extremism within their local communities and on campus can be instructive about how to actively participate in campus-based and off-campus events where free speech, protest, civic engagement, and civil rights overlap (Ahmadi & Cole, 2015; Ahmadi, Sanchez, & Cole, 2019). Student organizations can offer a collective, and sometimes supportive, space for students to learn, explore, and engage their racial and religious identities within the college or university context. Although student organizations can be as contentious as they can be supportive, peer groupings who share interests and marginalized social identities can impact students' sense of belonging, but also challenge the institution to be more responsive to their needs, experiences, and quality of educational experience. Although the burden of supporting students is not the primary responsibility of students, peer groups and student organizations can potentially be critical mediators in shaping both the positive and negative experiences of Black Muslim students (Schanzer, Kurzman, Toliver, & Miller, 2016).

The larger ramification for higher education institutions when Black Muslim students are supported and included within the fabric of the college milieu is that other students also are likely to benefit from these meaningful and institutionally supported interreligious and intraracial interactions (Ahmadi et al., 2019). Colleges and universities are also much closer to an enacted mission where diversity and inclusion are both valued and continuously pursued. Moreover, ongoing empirical research exploring and unearthing Black Muslim students' experiences with Islamophobia, racism, xenophobia, and sexism, as well as other "isms" becomes more desirable to better understand these students' unique and complex histories, institutional contexts, and college experiences. Access to both intellectual scholarship and this sort of empirically based data can reduce monolithic portrayals of Muslim students in general and Black Muslim students in particular. For instance, researchers and scholar-practitioners alike should investigate how policies at the nexus of CVE and Black Identity Extremism perpetuate Islamophobic perceptions and harmful professional practice on campus. Additionally, future research should include investigations of how postsecondary institutions negotiate *when* and *under what circumstances* to provide additional support to Black Muslim students within today's sociopolitical policy landscape, where exercising one's free speech and participating in social protest on and off campus occur frequently.

Conclusion

This chapter introduced the erasure of U.S. Congress Representative Ilhan Omar's racial identity as a Black women in order to highlight her Muslim identity. This manner of labeling one marginalized identity at the expense of another undermines intersectional perspectives. Through this example, we argue that grappling with and understanding the intersectionality of Black Muslims and by extension Black Muslim college students and exploring their experiences are critical for understanding Islamophobia and how Islamophobia is institutionalized through policies that coalesce to create multiple spheres of disparate impact. Moreover, without intersectional perspectives, monolithic portrayals of what it means to be Black and what it means to be Muslim are at best maintained and at worst used to (a) substantiate intraracial and intrareligious debates about inequities and (b) serve as a rationale for continuing the oppression Olympics. In either case, a lack of intersectional perspective undermines multiple perspective-taking, coalition building, and a close analysis of how power and privilege manifest through institutionalized policies and professional practice that do not serve the best interest of Black Muslim college students.

We then offered some historical perspective before focusing on institutions of higher education, not only outlining how Black students and Black Muslim college students have been understood by existing literature but also offering how students who share this dynamic identity face unique challenges in college settings. Finally, we provided recommendations for practitioners to suggest how postsecondary systems can better support the needs of Black Muslim students in ways that recognize their unique histories, contexts, and experiences.

Discussion Questions

1. Why is understanding the intersectionality of Black Muslim students' identities important? How does the oppression Olympics add to this perspective?

2. What are key moments within the American historical context that help give perspective to the experience of Black Muslims?

3. Describe the intersecting relationship between CVE and Black Identity Extremism on Black Muslims. How might this have ramifications for Black Muslim college students?

4. Given the recommendations provided previously, how might you use these suggestions or create others to improve the experiences of Black Muslim students on campus?

References

Ahmadi, S. (2011). The erosion of civil rights: Exploring the effects of the Patriot Act on Muslims in American higher education. *Rutgers Race and the Law Review*, *12*(1), 1–55.

Ahmadi, S., & Cole, D. (2015). Engaging religious minority students. In S. J. Quaye & S. Harper (Eds.), *Student engagement in higher education* (2nd ed., pp. 171–185). New York, NY: Routledge.

Ahmadi, S., Cole, D., & Prado, M. (2018). Understanding Islamophobia on college campuses. In M. Gasman & A. C. Samayoa (Eds.), *Contemporary issues in higher education* (pp. 135–152). New York, NY: Routledge.

Ahmadi, S., Sanchez, M., & Cole, D. (2019). Protecting Muslim students' speech and expression and resisting Islamophobia. In D. L. Morgan & C. H. Davis, III (Eds.), *Student activism, politics, and campus climate in higher education* (pp. 97–111). New York, NY: Routledge.

Ainsley, J. E., Volz, D., & Cooke, K. (2017). Exclusive: Trump to focus counter-extremism program solely on Islam. *Reuters*. Retrieved from https://www.reuters.com/article/us-usa-trump-extremists-program-exclusiv/exclusive-trump-to-focus-counter-extremism-program-solely-on-islam-sources-idUSKBN15G5VO

Amon, A. (2017, November 17). *African Muslims in early America*. Retrieved from https://nmaahc.si.edu/explore/stories/collection/african-muslims-early-america

Anapol, A. (2019, January 7). Muslim, black congresswomen pose for photo together: "Representation matters." *The Hill*. Retrieved from https://thehill.com/homenews/house/424209-muslim-congresswoman-and-black-congresswoman-share-photo-together

Aronson, J., Fried, C. B., & Good, C. (2002). Reducing the effects of stereotype threat on African American college students by shaping theories of intelligence. *Journal of Experimental Social Psychology*, *38*(2), 113–125.

Austin, A. D. (2012). *African Muslims in antebellum America: Transatlantic stories and spiritual struggles*. New York, NY: Routledge.

Beydoun, K. (2014). Antebellum Islam. *Howard Law Journal*, *58*(1), 141–193.

Beydoun, K., & Hansford, J. (2017). The FBI's dangerous crackdown on "Black identity extremists." *New York Times Online.* Retrieved from https://www .nytimes.com/2017/11/15/opinion/black-identity-extremism-fbi-trump.html

Black Lives Matter. (2018). *Herstory.* Retrieved from https://blacklivesmatter.com/ about/herstory/

Blaine, B., & Crocker, J. (1995). Religiousness, race, and psychological well-being: Exploring social psychological mediators. *Personality & Social Psychology Bulletin, 21*(10), 1031–1041.

Brown, M. C., & Davis, J. E. (2001). The Historically Black College as social contract, social capital, and social equalizer. *Peabody Journal of Education, 76*(1), 31–49.

Byars-Winston, A. M. (2006). Racial ideology in predicting social cognitive career variables for Black undergraduates. *Journal of Vocational Behavior, 69*(1), 134–148.

Cho, S., Crenshaw, K. W., & McCall, L. (2013). Toward a field of intersectionality studies: Theory, applications, and praxis. *Signs, 38*(4), 785–810.

Christian, M. D., & Barbarin, O. A. (2001). Cultural resources and psychological adjustment of African American children: Effects of spirituality and racial attribution. *Journal of Black Psychology, 27*, 43–63.

Cole, D., & Griffin, K. A. (2013). Advancing the study of student-faculty interaction: A focus on diverse students and faculty. In M. B. Paulsen (Ed.), *Higher education: Handbook of theory and research* (Vol. 28, pp. 561–611). Dordrecht, The Netherlands: Springer.

Constantine, M. G., Lewis, E. L., Conner, L. C., & Sanchez, D. (2000). Addressing spiritual and religious issues in counseling African Americans: Implications for counselor training and practice. *Counseling and Values, 45*, 28–39.

Constantine, M. G., Miville, M. L., Warren, A. K., Gainor, K. A., & Lewis-Coles, M. E. L. (2006). Religion, spirituality, and career development in African American college students: A qualitative inquiry. *The Career Development Quarterly, 54*(3), 227–241.

Crenshaw, K. (1991). Mapping the margins: Intersectionality, identity politics, and violence against women of color. *Stanford Law Review, 43*(6), 1241–1299.

Curtis, E. E. (2012). *Islam in Black America: Identity, liberation, and difference in African-American Islamic thought.* Albany, NY: SUNY Press.

Diouf, S. A. (1998). *Servants of Allah: African Muslims enslaved in the Americas.* New York, NY: New York University Press.

Executive Office of the President of the United States. (2011a). *Empowering local partners to prevent violent extremism in the United States.* Retrieved from https:// www.dhs.gov/sites/default/files/publications/empowering_local_partners.pdf

Executive Office of the President of the United States. (2011b). *Strategic implementation plan for empowering local partners to prevent violent extremism in the United States.* Retrieved from https://obamawhitehouse.archives.gov/sites/default/files/ sip-final.pdf

Federal Bureau of Investigation. (2005). *Terrorism 2002–2005*. Retrieved from https://www.fbi.gov/stats-services/publications/terrorism-2002-2005

Federal Bureau of Investigation, Intelligence Assessment, Counterterrorism Division. (2017). *Black identity extremists likely motivated to target law enforcement officers*. Retrieved from https://assets.documentcloud.org/documents/4067711/BIE-Redacted.pdf

Good, J., Halpin, G., & Halpin, G. (2002). Retaining black students in engineering: Do minority programs have a longitudinal impact? *Journal of College Student Retention: Research, Theory & Practice, 3*(4), 351–364.

Green, E. (2017, March 11). Muslim Americans are united by Trump—and divided by race. *Atlantic*. Retrieved from https://www.theatlantic.com/politics/archive/2017/03/muslim-americans-race/519282/

Grier-Reed, T. (2013). The African American Student Network: An informal networking group as a therapeutic intervention for black college students on a predominantly white campus. *Journal of Black Psychology, 39*(2), 169–184.

Griffin, K. A., Cunningham, E. L., & George Mwangi, C. A. (2016). Defining diversity: Ethnic differences in Black students' perceptions of racial climate. *Journal of Diversity in Higher Education, 9*(1), 34–49.

Hancock, A. M. (2011). *Solidarity politics for millennials: A guide to ending the oppression Olympics*. New York, NY: Palgrave Macmillan.

Harper, S. R. (2006). *Black male students at public flagship universities in the US: Status, trends, and implications for policy and practice*. Washington, DC: Joint Center for Political and Economic Studies, Health Policy Institute.

Helfstein, S., Abdullah, N., & al-Obaidi, M. (2009). *Deadly vanguards: A study of al-Qa'ida's violence against Muslims*. West Point, NY: Combating Terrorism Center at West Point. Retrieved from https://ctc.usma.edu/app/uploads/2010/10/deadly-vanguards_complete_l.pdf

Herndon, M. K. (2003). Expressions of spirituality among African-American college males. *The Journal of Men's Studies, 12*(1), 75–84.

Higgins, T. (2018, June). Supreme Court rules that Trump's travel ban is constitutional. *CNBC*. Retrieved from https://www.cnbc.com/2018/06/26/supreme-court-rules-in-trump-muslim-travel-ban-case.html

Johnson, S. C., & Arbona, C. (2006). The relation of ethnic identity, racial identity, and race-related stress among African American college students. *Journal of College Student Development, 47*(5), 495–507.

Khabeer, S. A. A. (2016). *Muslim cool: Race, religion, and hip hop in the United States*. New York, NY: NYU Press.

Lincoln, C. E. (1961). *The Black Muslims in America* (1st ed.). Boston, MA: Beacon.

Lincoln, C. E. (1994). *The Black Muslims in America* (3rd ed.). Grand Rapids, MI: Wm. B. Eerdmans.

Lundberg, C. A., & Schreiner, L. A. (2004). Quality and frequency of faculty-student interaction as predictors of learning: An analysis by student race/ethnicity. *Journal of College Student Development, 45*(5), 549–565.

Mamiya, L. H. (1982). From Black Muslim to Bilalian: The evolution of a movement. *Journal for the Scientific Study of Religion, 21*(2), 138–152.

Matthews, S., & Cyril, M. (2017). We say black lives matter. The FBI says that makes us a security threat. *Washington Post.* Retrieved from https://www.washingtonpost.com/news/posteverything/wp/2017/10/19/we-say-black-lives-matter-the-fbi-says-that-makes-us-a-security-threat/?utm_term=.c28cab9d58de

McGuire, K. M., Casanova, S., & Davis, C. H., III. (2016). "I'm a Black female who happens to be Muslim": Multiple marginalities of an immigrant Black Muslim woman on a predominantly white campus. *The Journal of Negro Education, 85*(3), 316–329.

Mohamed, B., & Diamant, J. (2019, January 17). Black Muslims account for a fifth of all U.S. Muslims, and about half are converts to Islam. *Factank.* Retrieved from http://www.pewresearch.org/fact-tank/2019/01/17/black-muslims-account-for-a-fifth-of-all-u-s-muslims-and-about-half-are-converts-to-islam/

Muhammad, R. (2013). *Muslims and the making of America: 1600s–present.* Los Angeles, CA: Muslim Public Affairs Council. Retrieved from https://virtuecenter.s3.amazonaws.com/files/2013-02-08-10/Muslims-and-the-Making-of-America.pdf

Patel, F., & Koushik, M. (2017). *Countering violent extremism.* New York, NY: Brennan Center for Justice, New York University School of Law. Retrieved from https://www.brennancenter.org/sites/default/files/publications/Brennan%20Center%20CVE%20Report_0.pdf

Patton, L. D. (2006). The voice of reason: A qualitative examination of black student perceptions of black culture centers. *Journal of College Student Development, 47*(6), 628–646.

Pew Research Center. (2016). *Religion and education around the world.* Retrieved from http://www.pewforum.org/2016/12/13/religion-and-education-around-the-world/

Pew Research Center. (2017a). *The changing global religious landscape.* Retrieved from http://www.pewforum.org/2017/04/05/the-changing-global-religious-landscape/

Pew Research Center. (2017b). *U.S. Muslims concerned about their place in society, but continue to believe in the American dream.* Retrieved from http://www.pewforum.org/2017/07/26/findings-from-pew-research-centers-2017-survey-of-us-muslims/

Phillips, F. L. S. (2000). *The effects of spirituality on the adjustment to college of African American students who attend a predominantly White institution* (Doctoral dissertation). Retrieved from Boston College Dissertations and Theses. (AAI9961582).

Riggins, R. K., McNeal, C., & Herndon, M. K. (2008). The role of spirituality among African-American college males attending a historically Black university. *College Student Journal, 42*(1), 70–82.

Robinson-Wood, T. L. (2009). Love, school, and money: Stress and cultural coping among ethnically diverse Black college women: A mixed-method analysis. *The Western Journal of Black Studies, 33*(2), 77–86.

Sahgal, N., & Smith, G. (2009, January 30). *A religious portrait of African-Americans.* Retrieved from http://www.pewforum.org/2009/01/30/a-religious-portrait-of-african-americans/

Sanchez, D. (2013). Racial and ego identity development in Black Caribbean college students. *Journal of Diversity in Higher Education, 6*(2), 115–126.

Sandoval-Lucero, E., Maes, J. B., & Klingsmith, L. (2014). African American and Latina(o) community college students' social capital and student success. *College Student Journal, 48*(3), 522–534.

Schanzer, D., Kurzman, C., Toliver, J., & Miller, E. (2016). *The challenge and promise of using community policing strategies to prevent violent extremism: A call for community partnerships with law enforcement to enhance public safety.* Durham, NC: Triangle Center on Terrorism and Homeland Security, Sanford School of Public Policy, Duke University.

Solorzano, D., Ceja, M., & Yosso, T. (2000). Critical race theory, racial microaggressions, and campus racial climate: The experiences of African American college students. *The Journal of Negro Education, 69*(1/2), 60–73.

Strayhorn, T. L. (2008). The role of supportive relationships in facilitating African American males' success in college. *NASPA Journal, 45*(1), 26–48.

Strayhorn, T. L. (2014). What role does grit play in the academic success of black male collegians at predominantly white institutions? *Journal of African American Studies, 18*(1), 1–10.

Strayhorn, T. L., Terrell, M. C., Redmond, J. S., & Walton, C. N. (2012). A home away from home: Black cultural centers as supporting environments for African American collegians at White institutions. In T. L. Strayhorn & M. C. Terrell (Eds.), *The evolving challenges of black college students: New insights for policy, practice, and research* (pp. 122–137). Sterling, VA: Stylus Publishing.

Tichavakunda, A. A. (2017). Perceptions of financial aid: Black students at a predominantly white institution. *Educational Forum, 81*(1), 3–17.

USA PATRIOT Act: Preserving life and liberty: Uniting and strengthening America by providing appropriate tools required to intercept and obstruct terrorism, Pub. L. No. 107-56, 115 Stat. 272 (2001). https://www.justice.gov/archive/ll/highlights.htm

Walker, K. L., & Dixon, V. (2002). Spirituality and academic performance among African American college students. *Journal of Black Psychology, 28*(2), 107–121.

Williamson, J. A. (1999). In defense of themselves: The black student struggle for success and recognition at predominantly white colleges and universities. *Journal of Negro Education, 68*(1), 92–105.

Wood, L., & Harris, F. (2015). The effect of academic engagement on sense of belonging: A hierarchical, multilevel analysis of black men in community colleges. *Spectrum: A Journal on Black Men, 4*(1), 21–47.

Zogby, J. (2015). CVE in the US: More harm than good. *Huffington Post.* Retrieved from https://www.huffingtonpost.com/james-zogby/cve-in-the-us-more-harm-t_b_7868180.html

7

LATINX MUSLIMS

Mabel Sanchez and Shafiqa Ahmadi

> *There are former Pentecostals and Catholics, Jehovah's Witnesses and agnostics, atheists and Mormons; they've all converted to Islam. They are from Puerto Rico and Mexico, Argentina and Ecuador, San Francisco and San Salvador, New York, Newark, Miami, and Houston. They are Latinx Muslims, one of the fastest growing religious communities in the U.S.*

—Ken Chitwood, "Why the Stories of Latinx Muslims Matter," February 1, 2018

Latinxs and Muslims are often portrayed as two mutually exclusive groups that do not fit within America's Black-White racial binary. The perceived commonalities between the two groups are of not belonging in American society and their supposed threat to the community. These narratives stem from a nativist perspective, and individuals who identify as Latinx or Muslim are forced to navigate and challenge a society that misunderstands and misrepresents them.

Although Latinxs and Muslims are portrayed as mutually exclusive groups in media and by the government, some individuals identify as both Latinx and Muslim. This group faces misunderstandings from American society, from the broader Latinx community, and from the larger Muslim community. This chapter (a) provides a brief history of Latinxs in the United States, including their conversion or reversion journey to Islam, and their interactions with their families; (b) discusses Latinx Muslim U.S. experiences; (c) describes the racialization of these two groups as the "brown threat" in America and the policies that have been instituted against them; and (d) addresses Latinx Muslims in higher education. This chapter concludes with recommendations and discussion questions.

Latinx Muslim History in the United States

Islam is the fastest growing religion in the United States (Ahmed & Reddy, 2007). Researchers estimate that Latinx Muslims are one of the fastest growing sectors of Islam in the United States (Lawton, 2014). In 2011, the Pew Research Center estimated that 6.4% of Muslims identified as Latinx (Pew Research Center, 2011). Bowen (2013) reports that there are around 200,000 Latinx Muslims in the United States. Later in 2014, Pew estimated that 4% of the Muslim population identified as Latinx (Pew Research Center, 2014). Quantifying the number of Latinxs who identify as Muslim is difficult because there is no record accounting for religious identification and mosques do not keep a record of membership.

Latinx Muslims are not a new phenomenon or trend. A significant number of Latinx Muslims converted from Catholicism, but some have identified as Muslims for several generations (Martínez-Vázquez, 2010). Researchers estimate that the number of Latinx Muslims is growing as this group continues to have children, especially because Latinxs are the fastest growing ethnic minority in the United States (Martínez-Vázquez, 2010). Latinx Muslims are spread throughout the United States and are from various countries across Mexico, Central America, South America, and the Caribbean (Ahmed & Reddy, 2007). Latinx Muslims primarily reside in large metropolitan cities such as New York, Los Angeles, and Chicago.

In the early 1900s, Latinxs in the United States were exposed to Islam through solidarity with the African American Muslim community and through marriage. This exposure led many Latinxs to become interested in Islam, convert, and later make efforts to spread Islam within the Latinx community. In order to help support the Latinx converts, Latinx Muslim organizations were born to meet the language and cultural needs of the Latinx community.

Early Latinx converts became associated with African American Muslim groups through the Moorish Science Temple established in the 1920s (Bowen, 2013). Bowen (2013) explains that these converts were attracted to the African American Muslim community because they promoted social justice issues centered around racism. At that time, Latinxs were facing similar issues of discrimination and racism and, therefore, found a sense of solidarity within the African American Muslim community. In the 1960s, Manuel 2X became one of the first Latinxs to spread the teachings of the Nation of Islam to Mexicans and Native Americans throughout Southern California (Bowen, 2013).

In addition to the relationship with the Moorish Science Temple, Latinxs came in contact with Islam through marriages with Muslim immigrants. Starting around the 1920s, Muslim men immigrated to the United States from South Asia, Yemen, and Palestine (Bowen, 2013). These men often came to the United States without wives, and the women of their countries typically stayed behind. Once the men were in the United States, they married Mexican women because racism and antimiscegenation practices of the time prohibited individuals from marrying those of different skin colors (Bowen, 2013).

The civil rights movement and other ethnic-nationalist identity movements of the 1960s and 1970s seemed to have inspired Latinx Muslims to create their own organization that would address their linguistic and cultural needs as their community grew. By 1975 the Alianza Islamica was established in Harlem (Bowen, 2013). The Alianza became a community center primarily with Islamic resources in Spanish for the Latinx community. The Alianza members continued to meet at the center for several years until the group dissolved in the mid-1990s; by that time, other Latinx Muslim organizations had been established (Bowen, 2013).

As Latinxs in the United States continued converting to Islam, there was a need for Latinx Muslim organizations that would support their cultural and linguistic needs. In 1982 the Association of Latin American Muslims was established after several Mexicans embraced Islam in North America and Europe (Bowen, 2013). This association began publishing *The Voice of Islam/ La Voz de Islam*, a bilingual monthly magazine, and distributed it throughout Spain and the Americas. Through this publication, other Latinx were able to learn about Islam in Spanish and later convert. In 1982, the Bism Rabbik Foundation was established by African American Muslims to provide accurate information regarding Islam in both English and Spanish (Bowen, 2013). The foundation produced the *Alianza Islamica*, another bilingual periodical, and did *da'wah*, or proselytization, in Latin American countries (Bowen, 2013). They hoped to provide more information and support to Spanish speakers across the Americas. Later in the 1980s, Propagación Islámica para la Educación e la Devoción a Alá' el Divino (PIEDAD) was also founded, and they began collaborating with the Islamic Circle of North America (ICNA) (Bowen, 2013). Many of these organizations focused on producing Islamic materials in Spanish and making them available to the Latinx community to help them better understand Islam for themselves. Bowen (2013) reports that by 1988 at least five organizations for Latinx Muslims were established in the United States. In 1997, the Latinx American Dawah Organization (LADO) was formed and today continues to collaborate with other Latinx Muslim organizations (Bowen, 2013).

At times Latinx Muslims experienced pushback when trying to form Latinx organizations because some feared that it would cause division within the broader Muslim community (Bowen, 2013). However, through these organizations, Latinx Muslims have found support for their faith, their ethnic identity, their preferred language, and other issues related to the Latinx community. Before the establishment of Latinx Muslim organizations, some Latinxs found it difficult to feel part of the broader Muslim community. They felt excluded from certain practices for lack of linguistic understanding of Islamic texts, and in some cases, they have felt excluded for being converts (Martínez-Vázquez, 2010). The Latinx organizations, however, have offered support to a Latinx Muslim community that has often struggled with immigration issues and racism as well as provided information about Islam in Spanish (Bowen, 2013; Galvan, 2008). Latinx Muslim organizations have helped the Muslim Latinx community better explain their faith to their family members and other community members who often think that not being Catholic is a part of abandoning or rejecting Latinx culture (Bowen, 2013; Galvan, 2008; Martínez-Vázquez, 2010).

Conversion or Reversion to Islam

Many Latinxs have converted or reverted to Islam throughout the years. Sometimes the terms *converted* and *reverted* are used interchangeably, but they indicate a different connection to the Islamic religion. In Islam, it is believed that everyone is Muslim at birth. When Latinxs and others who did not grow up Muslim choose to be Muslim later in life, they see it as a reversion to their original religion (Martínez-Vázquez, 2010). Some Latinx Muslims converse with their family members and tell them that they were always Muslim without knowing it (Martínez-Vázquez, 2010). They often tell their family members that a lot of the customs and traditions within Latinx culture stem from Islam because both groups have similar values (Martínez-Vázquez, 2010). Conversion alludes more to a decision to choose to enter into a religion that was not the original or initial religion of the individual. Often, Latinx Muslims are referred to as converts by the broader Muslim community and sometimes excluded based on their cultural and linguistic needs (Bowen, 2013; Martínez-Vázquez, 2010). Those who write about the Latinx Muslim experience often write from a conversion perspective, but many Latinx Muslims talk about their experience from a reversion perspective.

As Latinx Muslims have reverted to Islam, they have found ways to historically connect their identity to Islam by looking back to the Moors in Spain (Bowen, 2013; Martínez-Vázquez, 2010, 2012). Many explain their conversion or reversion as a return to their pre-Hispanic and pre-Catholic identity. This examination of history connects them to Muslim Spain, which provides a link to Muslims in Latin America as the Spanish colonized Latin America (Martínez-Vásquez, 2010, 2012). Latinx Muslims engage in an identity reconstruction process that will justify or legitimize both their ethnic and religious identity without lessening or threatening a piece of who they are.

In reverting back to Islam, Latinx Muslims disrupt the normative view of Latinxs for both Latinx families and the broader American society (Martínez-Vásquez, 2012). In 2014, Pew estimated that 80% of Latinxs identified as Catholic, Protestant, or another Christian faith. Many of the traditional views of Latinxs center around a Christian (Catholic) religious paradigm mixed with *mestizaje*, the indigenous and Spanish children of Latin America (Martínez-Vásquez, 2012). This paradigm, however, completely ignores Muslim voices as well as other races within the Latinx community. Mitú (2016), a Latinx digital media company, challenged this paradigm by releasing a video depicting an Afro-Latina who reverted to Islam when she was 20 years old. This depiction shatters the normative view of *latinidad* in America as the video shows a phenotypically Black woman in Mexican-style dress also wearing a hijab. Although she does not depict the perceived norm of being Latina, she emphasizes that the Latinx community is diverse and that she, too, is part of the Latinx culture.

Those who revert must find a way to explain that their newfound Muslim identity is not in conflict with their *latinidad*; rather, their ethnicity fits within the larger Muslim religious group (Martínez-Vázquez, 2012). Martínez-Vázquez (2010) interviewed a group of Latinxs who had reverted to Islam. In several cases, these Latinx Muslims expressed feeling alienated from their broader Latinx community. Although religion is not fixed, for the Latinx community, religious practices become tradition, therefore making it seem as though religion is fixed within the Latinx community (Martínez-Vázquez, 2012). When some Latinxs reverted to Islam and left the Catholic Church or other Christian denomination, some experienced pushback from their families who saw this change in religion as a betrayal of Latinx tradition and culture.

Muslim Latinx often felt alienated during family gatherings for having different religious beliefs and different social practices. Drinking alcohol and eating pork dishes are central to the social aspect of Latinx community and family gatherings (Martínez-Vázquez, 2010); however, many Muslims have chosen not to eat pork or drink alcohol for religious reasons. Because there was a change in their eating habits and behaviors, some Latinx Muslims stopped attending family gatherings to prevent uncomfortable situations and conversations (Martínez-Vázquez, 2010). Reichard (2015) interviewed five Muslim Latinas who reverted to Islam regarding their experiences with their families during Easter, a Christian holiday and family celebration. They reported experiencing conflict with their families who either tried to "save" them from Islam or would try to feed them pork and other non-*halal* food items (Reichard, 2015). The changes in habits caused family members to question converts' *latinidad* and commitment to the family (Lawton, 2014; Martínez-Vázquez, 2010, 2012).

In reverting to Islam, many Latinxs had to reconstruct their identity to find the cultural similarities between Muslim practices and Latinx culture. Part of this reconstruction of identity is learning about the Moors in Spain (Bowen, 2013; Lawton, 2014; Martínez-Vázquez, 2010, 2012). Many see Islam as part of their past and even point to the Arabic influence on certain Spanish words such as *almohada, algebra*, and *pantalón* (Bowen, 2013; Martínez-Vásquez, 2010, 2012). Latinx Muslims link their religion and culture through values and teachings regarding the importance of family (Martínez-Vásquez, 2010, 2012). Martínez-Vásquez (2010) interviewed a woman who would tell her male relatives that they were already Muslim, that they just did not know it, but that their family values and culture stemmed from Islam's teachings.

Latinx Muslims' Experiences in the United States

Muslims are subjected to various forms of discrimination in the United States. Records estimated that in 2017 anti-Muslim assaults surpassed the number of anti-Muslim assaults in 2001 (Kishi, 2017). Most information and data about Muslim discrimination are presented as a broad categorization, ignoring the various racial and ethnic backgrounds within the Muslim community. Zainiddinov (2016) argues that it is important to understand if different racial and ethnic groups experience discrimination similarly or differently. Understanding the experiences of Latinx Muslims can be complicated even if the larger Muslim population is disaggregated by race or ethnicity. The Latinx or Hispanic group is not considered a race within the United States; it is regarded as an ethnicity because Latinxs can have Black, Asian, White, and Native American heritage (Alcoff, 2012). Goldberg (1993) suggested using the term *ethnorace* for identity groups for which *race* and *ethnicity* have been used interchangeably. Gallup (2009) conducted a survey in which the racial demographics only include White, Black, Asian, and Other. They reported that only 1% of Muslims in the study volunteered "Hispanic" as their answer, which indicates that the option was not initially given, but respondents felt the need to make this distinction. The respondents who volunteered "Hispanic" did not immediately identify with any of the racial categories provided. These kinds of categories on surveys and other data-collecting tools present an issue in giving an accurate number of Latinxs and, therefore, Latinx Muslims, making it more difficult to understand their experiences.

Zainiddinov (2016) used data from the Pew Research Center (2011) to explore the discrimination faced by Muslims of different racial and ethnic groups. The data set included five racial/ethnic identity categories: Black, non-Hispanic; Asian, non-Hispanic; Hispanic; White, non-Hispanic; and other or mixed. Zainiddinov (2016) found that out of the five racial/ethnic categories used, Hispanics were the group that most often perceived discrimination overall and in the four categories measured (Pew Research Center, 2011). Hispanics perceived that people were suspicious of them, were called offensive names and singled out by law enforcement, and were physically threatened and attacked due to one or more of their identities more than any other racial or ethnic group. Latinx Muslims were more likely to face and report discrimination in the United States than White Muslims, Black Muslims, and Asian Muslims (Zainiddinov, 2016). Latinxs may face discrimination due to their ethnic minority status, their religious affiliation, or a combination of both (Zainiddinov, 2016). In addition to experiencing discrimination from the larger American population, Latinx Muslims face discrimination from the broader Latinx and Muslim communities (Ahmed & Reddy, 2007; Bowen, 2013; Galvan, 2008; Martínez-Vázquez, 2010; Zainiddinov, 2016). For instance, the broader Latinx community often discriminates against Latinx Muslims for converting to Islam and seemingly abandoning Latinx values centered on Catholicism (Ahmed & Reddy, 2007; Bowen, 2013; Galván, 2008; Martínez-Vázquez, 2010; Zainiddinov, 2016). The broader Muslim community discriminates against Latinx Muslims for being converts and not being from Muslim countries (Bowen, 2013; Galvan, 2008; Martínez-Vázquez, 2010).

Muslims experience discrimination in all aspects of their life, including the workplace, school, and leisure (Zainiddinov, 2016). Muslims experience verbal abuse, physical threats, religious profiling, and racial profiling, which may cause psychological stress (Ahmed & Reddy, 2007; Zainiddinov, 2016). Ahmed and Reddy (2007) describe immigrant Muslims and indigenous or American Muslims in their analysis. Researchers suggest that Muslim immigrants in the United States experience psychological distress such as anxiety, depression, and posttraumatic stress disorder due to feelings of discrimination and alienation (Ahmed & Reddy, 2007; Hedayat-Diba, 2000). The immigrant Muslims, although not defined, seem to come from

Middle Eastern countries (a term constructed by Western/orientalist scholars based on geopolitical interests/perspectives using a wide geographical area spanning from Morocco to Indonesia). *Middle Eastern, Middle Easterners*, or the *Middle East* are used often in literature. Ahmed and Reddy (2007) also discuss Hispanic or Latinx Muslims and consider them indigenous or American Muslims. The indigenous or American Muslim group faces psychological stressors of family tension, guilt, and identity issues (Ahmed & Reddy, 2007). However, this interpretation ignores that many Latinx families are also immigrant families within the United States. Therefore, Latinx Muslims can experience psychological stressors for being immigrants and not being native to the Americas. Latinx Muslims are subject to both types of psychological stressors and alienation, from not only the larger American society but also their own families.

As Latinxs convert to Islam, many family members become upset and confused, which causes tension in their relationships. For Latinxs who attended Catholic schools and convert to Islam, their parents can express discomfort and guilt that they had somehow not raised their children "right" (Lawton, 2014; Martínez-Vázquez, 2010; Reichard, 2015). Some Latinx parents and siblings stopped talking to the family member who was now Muslim for some time because they had a hard time understanding their religious choice (Lawton, 2014; Martínez-Vázquez, 2010; Reichard, 2015). This conflict with their families caused some Latinx Muslims to feel alone, especially during Muslim holidays (Martínez-Vázquez, 2010; Reichard, 2015). Although they wanted to respect their families, they also wanted their faith to be respected.

Many Latinx families did not have proper exposure to Islam before the conversion of their family members. In 2010, Telemundo, a Spanish network, aired the remake of *El Clon*, a very successful telenovela that was initially aired in Brazil and often makes it on lists of "must watch telenovelas." Commentators describe *El Clon* as "a contemporary story of love and honor that deals with such topics as drug trafficking, cloning and attitudes to Islam" (Brennan, 2008, para. 8). *Latin Post* classifies *El Clon* as one of the "6 Best Telenovelas of All Time" and provides the plotline:

> Jade . . . moves to Morocco with her uncle Ali after her mother dies. Being used to a liberal lifestyle, Jade must convert to Islam and its strict laws towards women. . . . Jade is not allowed to date outside of Islam so she and Lucas [her lover] plan to escape Morocco together. (Santiago, 2014, para. 16)

Although *El Clon* often receives high reviews, it is a problematic portrayal of Islam. The description and the storyline depict Islam as an oppressive religion to women, and thus, Jade and Lucas must escape to find happiness and true love. *El Clon* is one of the few depictions of Islam in Spanish (or Portuguese) that Latinxs have access to, and it both creates a negative portrayal and fear of Islam and further perpetuates the stereotypes that some in the Latinx community have about Islam and Muslims.

Furthermore, because of the stereotypical portrayal of Islam and Muslims by the media, families of Latinx Muslims worry about the way others might treat their family members. Families of Latinx women who decided to wear a hijab worry about their visible religiosity and have often begged them to take it off or asked when they were going to take it off (Martínez-Vázquez, 2010; Reichard, 2015). The families worried that they would become easy targets of discrimination due to the negative narratives about Islam that were spread post-9/11.

Latinx Muslims do not just become the target of discrimination in their daily interactions; they have also become targets of the government. In the Trump administration, Latinx Muslims' multiple and intersecting identities are targeted and discriminated against. *Noticias Telemundo* (2016) interviewed a Mexican Muslim woman who reported feeling triply at risk during the Trump administration for having "las tres *M's*—Musulmana, Mujer, y Mexicana," or being Muslim, female, and Mexican. Trump and his administration have spoken of these groups negatively and even criminalized them through his policies. Much of this adverse treatment and negative impact of policies can also impact higher education spaces.

The Brown Threat

During the 2016 presidential election, Donald Trump targeted and portrayed both the Muslim and Latinx communities as untrustworthy, criminals, and terrorists. Schneider and Ingram (1993) present a model on how target group identities are socially constructed and negatively portrayed by those in power. This model illustrates how political power and constructed social identities interact to create different classifications in society. Under Schneider and Ingram's (1993) model, both of these groups would classify as deviants. Neither Muslims nor Latinxs hold much power in the political spectrum and have negatively constructed identities. Alcoff (2012) states that nativism allows these "nonnative" groups to be viewed as a threat to the cohesion and tradition of America. This cohesion and the culture of America, however, is reserved for White America (i.e., those who are of European descent).

People and media often portray Latinxs and Muslims as the other, the foreigners who do not belong in American society or fit neatly within the American Black-White racial binary. Rivera (2014) describes both of these groups as the brown threat to American society. Post-9/11 discourses depicted Middle Eastern Muslims and Latinxs as a threat to Americans' social and economic well-being (Rivera, 2014). Throughout the years, narratives about Muslims and Latinxs depict them as threatening the safety of Americans or stealing jobs, therefore hurting the American economy. These narratives were and continue to be widely shared and circulated, creating a sense of fear among other Americans and spreading a negative construction of both groups.

Post-9/11, there was a bigger push for national security and for finding potential threats, which led the government to enact different measures. One act (Border Protection, Anti-Terrorism, and Illegal Immigration Control Act of 2005) sought to address

> border security vulnerabilities on land directly adjacent to the international borders of the United States under the jurisdiction of the Department of the Interior related to the prevention of the entry of terrorists, other unlawful aliens, narcotics, and other contraband into the United States. (Section 302a)

The language and goal of this act was to group immigrants and terrorists as undesired and a threat to American society (Kyriakides & Torres, 2015). Such policies and bills further construct negative identities for both Latinxs and Muslims (Schneider & Ingram, 1993), despite the many law-abiding Latinxs and Muslims who live in the United States.

Although this act did not explicitly say *Latinx*, the emphasis of this bill was on the U.S. southwest border, putting the focus on Latinx immigration. Deputy Secretary of Homeland Security Admiral James Loy introduced the bill before the U.S. Congress, saying,

> Emerging threat streams strongly suggest that al-Qaeda has considered using the southwest border to infiltrate the United States. Several al-Qaeda leaders believe operatives can pay their way into the country through Mexico and also believe illegal entry is more advantageous than legal entry for operational security reasons. However, there is currently no evidence that al-Qaeda operatives have made successful penetration into the United States via this method. (U.S. Congress Report, 2005, pp. 40–41)

The type of language used by the deputy secretary demonstrates the criminalization of Mexico and associates all Muslims with al-Qaeda without having actual evidence. Alcoff (2012) asserts that the attacks on immigration tend to be on Mexico and on those who look Mexican. Mexico, in the context of this act, is synonymous with Latinx and al-Qaeda with Muslims, which further extends the groups that are being otherized and classified as deviants and criminals (Schneider & Ingram, 1993).

During the presidential campaign and afterward, Trump targeted both Latinxs and Muslims and depicted both groups as a problem or threat to American society. Trump has labeled Latinxs as "bad *hombres*" and Muslims as terrorists, making them the undesirable brown groups of American society. During his campaign, Trump said,

> When Mexico sends its people, they're not sending their best. They're not sending you . . . they're not sending you . . . they're sending people that have lots of problems, and they're bringing those problems. . . . They're bringing drugs. They're bringing crime. They're rapists. And some, I assume, are good people. But I speak to border guards and they tell us what we're getting. And it only makes common sense. . . . They're sending us not the right people. It's coming from more than Mexico. It's coming from all over South and Latin America, and it's coming probably—probably—from the Middle East. But we don't know. Because we have no protection and we have no competence, we don't know what's happening. And it's got to stop and it's got to stop fast. (Trump, 2015, para. 4)

Without a shred of evidence, Trump spoke with a sense of urgency that immediately criminalized both Latinxs and people from the Middle East, who are all often thought of as being Muslim. In a single speech, he classified both groups as deviant brown threats to American society.

During the first year of Trump's administration, he proposed and signed three different versions of the travel ban that became known as the Muslim ban. President Trump issued the executive order with the reasoning that it would protect the nation from foreign terrorists by preventing their entry (White House, 2017). However, travel bans targeted Muslim-majority countries by restricting travel to and from these countries. In targeting Muslim-majority countries and framing it as a security issue, Trump identified Muslim people from those countries as a threat to American society.

In addition to targeting the Muslim community, Trump targeted the Latinx community from the beginning of his campaign. Trump talked about building a wall along the Mexican border and deporting "illegal" immigrants because there are too many "bad *hombres*." He framed the Latinx presence in the United States as a security issue that threatens the well-being of American society. Since Trump took office, deportations increased by 32.6% in the first few weeks of his administration (Sacchetti, 2017). The Deferred Action and

Childhood Arrival (DACA) program and the Temporary Protected Status (TPS) program have been challenged or ended.

Both DACA and TPS are supposed to help allow a select few to stay in the United States without the fear of deportation but do not provide a pathway to citizenship. DACA is an immigration policy that started under the Obama administration for those who had entered the country as children. To benefit, these individuals must have entered the country before their 16th birthday, have completed or be in the process of completing high school or the equivalent, and have been in good legal standing with no felonies and no more than 3 misdemeanors (U.S. Citizenship and Immigration Services, n.d.a). TPS started in 1990 and allowed individuals to temporarily reside in the United States due to unsafe conditions in their home country. Countries that are currently designated for TPS are El Salvador, Haiti, Honduras, Nepal, Nicaragua, Sudan, South Sudan, Syria, and Yemen (U.S. Citizenship and Immigration Services, n.d.b). Both programs protect from deportation and allow a work permit to beneficiaries. Beneficiaries must prove that they are deserving individuals by proving that they are in good legal standing. Since Trump challenged DACA, 122 people lose their protected status daily (Johnson, 2017). Additionally, it is estimated that nearly 300,000 people could lose their status if TPS ends (Murray, 2017).

Media and the government depict the Latinx community and the Muslim community as two separate communities that threaten American society and are often confused for each other. Some members of these communities have similar physical features such as skin and hair color that do not fit within the American Black-White racial binary (Rivera, 2014). Various television shows, cartoons, and comics have portrayed both groups as interchangeable as long as they wear the attire associated with their community. Although both communities are seen as mutually exclusive, they become united through the perceived or socially constructed "threat" that they present to American society. These groups are marginalized and singled out as the "other." These two groups' physical features, along with speaking English with an accent, often single them out as foreign and not fitting in American society, making them interchangeable (Rivera, 2014).

American society fails to recognize that there are Muslim Latinxs and that Islam and Latinxs are not mutually exclusive. Latinx Muslims would classify as doubly deviant for their religious identity and their ethnic identity (Schneider & Ingram, 1993). In failing to recognize that Latinxs and Muslims are not mutually exclusive identities, scholars have failed to understand the intersectionality of these groups' identities and experiences in American society (Martínez-Vásquez, 2010). In large part, some in the broader Muslim community have had to find ways to support and help Latinxs navigate the intersection of their identities as Latinx Muslims by providing them with educational materials in Spanish or by opening centers and organizations designated for Latinx Muslims (Martínez-Vásquez, 2010). In 2016, the first and only Spanish-program mosque for Latinxs opened in Houston (Schuessler, 2016).

Latinx and Muslim Experiences in Higher Education

Colleges and universities in the United States were founded to serve a particular population of White men. Colonies founded colleges tied to Christian denominations to educate and prepare White men for service and clergy work (Rudolph, 1962). Different colonies set up their own colleges as a "pursuit of denominational survival in an environment of religious diversity" (p. 8). "Religious diversity" referred to different Christian denominations and no other religions.

As colleges expanded west, they moved away from their religious ties and also allowed students of other races and ethnicities to enroll. Although more students were allowed to enroll in higher education institutions, their historical roots of exclusion were not always challenged but rather continued to be an underlying reality (Hurtado, Milem, Clayton-Pedersen, & Allen, 1999). The history of exclusion often permeated and continues to permeate the institutions, constantly reminding specific populations that these spaces were not intended for them (Hurtado et al., 1999).

Today, some institutions of higher education continue to be unwelcoming spaces for communities and groups who do not identify as White or Christian. Although some structures and programs on college campuses are deemed as "colorblind" or equal, they fail to recognize the unique needs of marginalized communities in higher education. In doing so, whiteness and Christianity continue to be the norm on college campuses, therefore excluding other communities. Institutions of higher education are not always welcoming spaces for Muslims or Latinxs, so when these identities intersect, there is even less support.

Muslim Student Experiences in Higher Education

Muslim college students face several aspects of Islamophobia on or near college campuses. They continue to be called terrorists or attacked for being Muslim. The USA PATRIOT Act (2001), signed by President Bush, helped create a sense of fear and hatred toward Muslims. In an effort to "protect" the nation, surveillance heightened and visas were revoked, even for scholars and college students (Ahmadi, 2011). Although the USA PATRIOT Act was supposed to increase security measures for everyone, it was mainly Muslims or those of Middle Eastern descent who were targeted and surveilled. Throughout the years, various students have expressed a sense of fear that the government is watching them due to their last names, visible markers such as wearing a hijab or having a beard and wearing a kufi, or involvement with a Muslim religious student group.

Muslim students do not feel as welcome or respected for their religious beliefs as they should. Nasir and Al-Amin (2006) wrote that "the practice of Islam in the college setting is at once intensely personal and painfully public" (p. 22). Although Muslims often explain Islam as a relationship with God, something deeply personal, some religious practices such as prayer, dress, and fasting make them very visible and identifiable on college campuses. Not all campuses provide spaces for students to pray or to practice their religion, forcing them to practice their religion in public spaces where they may not feel safe or comfortable (Nasir & Al-Amin, 2006). Although visibility may not be necessarily a bad thing, it becomes painful because it is a constant reminder of the lack of fit in the college community and how others misunderstand Islam (Cole & Ahmadi, 2003; Nasir & Al-Amin, 2006). There is a general lack of understanding regarding the unique needs of Muslim students on college campuses in all aspects of their college life (Cole & Ahmadi, 2003, 2010).

The hypervisibility of Muslims on college campuses contributes to their discomfort because they often feel that others view them negatively, which contributes to feelings of isolation (Hopkins, 2011). Some students express discomfort or fear of being called a terrorist when they want to practice their religion on campus (Nasir & Al-Amin, 2006). Others express feeling discomfort when others see them or think of them as an oppressed group (Cole & Ahmadi, 2003; Nasir & Al-Amin, 2006).

After Trump was elected president, there was a rise in the number of Islamophobic incidents on college campuses across the United States. The Islamophobic rhetoric in Trump's campaign contributed to these incidents. Muslim students were called names, attacked, and some had their hijabs yanked off their heads. In 2017, Pew found that Muslim millennials were less likely than older Muslims to say that Americans are friendly toward Muslims (Diamant & Gecewicz, 2017).

Latinx Experiences in Higher Education

Although campuses have become more racially and ethnically diverse, it is not sufficient to have a diverse physical presence but not have the appropriate structures to support different groups (Stotzer & Hossellman, 2012). Stotzer and Hossellman (2012) conducted a study looking at racial diversity and its impact on the number of reported hate crimes on campus. They reported that when schools were more successful in recruiting minority students such as Black and Latinx participants, students reported fewer hate crimes on campus. However, having an increased physical representation on campus and less reporting of hate crimes does not mean that Latinx students feel welcomed on campus. Additionally, hate crimes are an extreme, and students may be experiencing other forms of discrimination, such as microaggressions, that can be very harmful to a student's self-esteem and academic success (Minikel-Lacocque, 2013).

Latinx students in higher education often do not feel welcomed or that they belong in higher education institutions. Hurtado and Carter (1997) conducted a study that built on Tinto's (1993) concept of membership in college campus life as a predictor for departure. Students need to feel welcomed and a part of the campus environment to succeed academically and persist through graduation (Hurtado & Carter, 1997). Hurtado and Ponjuan (2005) conducted a study looking at the campus climate for Latinx students during their second year of college. In this study, they found "that students who retain strong cultural ties are less likely to see their university as a welcoming campus environment" (p. 244). Moreover, students who perceived negative campus climates reported a lower sense of belonging at their campus (Hurtado & Ponjuan, 2005). Minikel-Lacocque (2013) interviewed Latinx students as they transitioned into a predominantly White institution and found that they often felt isolated in their college community.

In addition to students feeling isolated and unwelcome in their college community, Latinx students had negative experiences that included racism, discrimination, and microaggressions. One of the students interviewed by Minikel-Lacocque (2013) said that he "sticks out more" (p. 448) due to his ethnicity. Some of these students were easily identifiable in the middle of a White community, which made them more prone to discrimination, ignorant remarks, stereotypes, racialized aggressions, and microaggressions (Minikel-Lacocque, 2013). Nadal, Wong, Griffin, Davidoff, and Sriken (2014) found that such experiences often negatively affected students' mental health and self-esteem. Although campuses admitted Latinxs, these students often did not feel they were adequately supported. Minikel-Lacocque (2013) recommended more programming and training regarding racism to begin supporting Latinx students as they transition into spaces that had denied access to people like them in the past.

Latinx Muslim Experiences in Higher Education

In 2017, Pew Research Center estimated that 11% of Muslim millennials identify as Hispanic (Diamant & Gecewicz, 2017). It is possible that the population of Latinx Muslims in higher education institutions is similar to that of Muslim millennials because most are within traditional college-going age. It is possible that this community also faces issues with access, much like the larger Latinx population. However, it is difficult to know how many Latinx Muslims there are in higher education institutions and any barriers they may face. Like the larger Latinx Muslim population, the Latinx Muslim college population has been severely understudied. The little information we have often comes from blogs, social media, and panels.

Given that both Muslim students and Latinx students express feelings of isolation and exclusion on their college campuses, it is safe to assume that Latinx Muslims are dually burdened and feel isolated and excluded. Hurtado and Carter (1997) wrote that membership in religious organizations is one of the most significant factors related to students' sense of belonging. Although membership in such organizations may be helpful, Latinx Muslims may have difficulties entering these spaces or feeling welcomed in them because they are not of Middle Eastern descent. The adults in Martínez-Vázquez's (2010) study expressed some sense of difficulty in exclusively Latinx spaces and exclusively Muslim spaces. These spaces often fail to recognize the complexity of their intersectional identities as Latinx Muslims. Muslims and Latinxs are often portrayed as two mutually exclusive groups. Islam is often thought of as a monoethnic religion made up of Middle Easterners, and Latinxs are often portrayed as belonging to one religion, Catholicism, which falls under the Christian umbrella. However, the Muslim population is ethnically diverse, and not all Latinxs are Catholic. There are Latinx Muslims, but they are often ignored by the media, the government, scholars, and institutions of higher education.

Recommendations

It is clear that scholars have largely ignored the Latinx Muslim population; often, so have their own communities. More research on the Latinx Muslim community to better understand their experiences in society at large and on college campuses is needed. The Latinx Muslim population is a unique group whose intersectional identities are important to explore and understand to provide better support.

The broader research community should focus on more research to understand the unique legal and political struggles that the Latinx Muslim community may be facing. Under the current political administration, various identities have been targeted; however, very little is known about the intersection of these targeted identities and the effects of these policies on individuals and their well-being.

College campuses and practitioners must incorporate better frameworks to support Latinx Muslim students' transition and integration into college. Both Muslim students and Latinx students feel isolated and lack a sense of belonging on their college campuses. If and when students hold both of these identities, it is highly probable that they too are feeling a sense of isolation and a lack of sense of belonging on their college campuses. Students may be experiencing stress and isolation due to their minority identities that American higher education has historically excluded from their campuses and master plans, and from a lack of fit in both of their communities. Like the adults who were interviewed by scholars like Martínez-Vásquez (2010), Latinx Muslims may have difficulties finding community within Latinx student groups and within Muslim student groups because they do not fit the perceived norm of these communities.

Conclusion

The Latinx Muslim community is an understudied and a complex population. Latinxs are the fastest growing ethnic minority in the United States and the fastest growing sector of Islam. Those who identify as Latinx Muslims are extremely diverse and come from a variety of countries. Some have converted to Islam, and others were born into Islam.

In public and political discourse, Latinxs and Muslims are framed as undesirable or threatening individuals to American society. Under Schneider and Ingram's (1993) view, Latinx Muslims would be doubly deviant in American society, thus becoming doubly exasperating in their undesirability in American society. This undesirability and fear have allowed for policies and laws to be passed and enacted that explicitly target Latinxs and Muslims without having concrete evidence to believe that they present a threat to the well-being of American society.

For those Latinxs who decide to convert into Islam, they must engage in reconstructing their identities and explaining their choices to their Latinx families. In a way, they do not fit with the broader Latinx community or with the larger Muslim community. Historically, this lack of fitting in sparked the need for specific Latinx Muslim organizations to provide Islamic materials in Spanish and help to navigate the reconstruction of identity. In reconstructing their identity, many look to the Moorish presence in Spain as a tie back to their roots. Reconstructing their identity is a way to not only preserve their *latinidad* but also identify as Muslim.

Unfortunately, not much is known regarding the Latinx Muslim population in college. Based on the trends and experiences of other Latinx Muslims, we assume that Latinx Muslim college students may be facing similar struggles of identity reconstruction and lack of fit. Additionally, these students may face challenges that Latinxs and Muslims face separately. Both groups express feelings of isolation on college campuses. These feelings may be further exacerbated by not being able to find an ethnic or religious community with which to identify at the college.

Further research is recommended regarding Latinx Muslims at all levels to better understand their experiences and provide better support. This can helps us to influence policy to better serve this community. Additionally, we may be able to help colleges provide better support for Latinx Muslims on campus. By doing so, feelings of isolation may decrease over time and academic success may increase.

Discussion Questions

1. What are the experiences of Latinx Muslim students on campus?
2. What are Latinx Muslim students' religious and cultural needs that college campuses can accommodate?
3. How can faculty and staff ensure inclusion of Latinx Muslim students?
4. How can institutions of higher education mitigate legal and political struggles that Latinx Muslim students face?

References

Ahmadi, S. (2011). The erosion of civil rights: Exploring the effects of the Patriot Act on Muslims in American higher education. *Rutgers Race & the Law Review*, *12*, 1–46.

Ahmed, S., & Reddy, L. A. (2007). Understanding the mental health needs of American Muslims: Recommendations and considerations for practice. *Journal of Multicultural Counseling and Development*, *35*(4), 207–218.

Alcoff, L. (2012). Anti-Latinx racism. In A. M. Isasi-Díaz & E. Mendieta (Eds.), *Decolonizing epistemologies: Latina/o theology and philosophy* (pp. 107–126). New York, NY: Fordham University Press.

Border Protection, Anti-Terrorism, and Illegal Immigration Control Act. (2005). HR 4437. Retrieved from https://www.gpo.gov/fdsys/pkg/BILLS-109hr4437rfs/pdf/BILLS-109hr4437rfs.pdf

Bowen, P. D. (2013). US Latina/o Muslims since 1920: From "Moors" to "Latinx Muslims." *Journal of Religious History, 37*(2), 165–184.

Brennan, S. (2008). Telemundo reincarnates "El clon." *Hollywood Reporter.* Retrieved from https://www.hollywoodreporter.com/news/telemundo-reincarnates-el-clon-111418

Chitwood, K. (2018). Why the stories of Latinx Muslims matter [Web log post]. Retrieved from http://www.kenchitwood.com/blog/2018/1/31/why-the-stories-of-latinx-muslims-matter

Cole, D., & Ahmadi, S. (2003). Perspectives and experiences of Muslim women who veil on college campuses. *Journal of College Student Development, 44*(1), 47–66.

Cole, D., & Ahmadi, S. (2010). Reconsidering campus diversity: An examination of Muslim students' experiences. *The Journal of Higher Education, 81*(2), 121–139.

Diamant, J., & Gecewicz, C. (2017). *5 facts about Muslim millennials in the U.S.* Retrieved from https://www.pewresearch.org/fact-tank/2017/10/26/5-facts-about-muslim-millennials-us/

Gallup. (2009). *Muslim Americans: A national portrait—An in-depth analysis of America's most diverse religious community.* Washington, DC: Gallup Press. Retrieved from http://www.themosqueinmorgantown.com/pdfs/GallupAmericanMuslimReport.pdf

Galvan, J. (2008). Who are Latinx Muslims? *Islamic Horizons, 37*(4), 26–30.

Goldberg, D. (1993). *Racist culture: Philosophy and the politics of meaning.* Cambridge, MA: Blackwell.

Hedayat-Diba, Z. (2000). Psychotherapy with Muslims. In P. S. Richards & A. E. Bergin (Eds.), *Handbook of psychotherapy and religious diversity* (pp. 289–314). Washington, DC: American Psychological Association.

Hopkins, P. (2011). Towards critical geographies of the university campus: Understanding the contested experiences of Muslim students. *Transactions of the Institute of British Geographers, 36*(1), 157–169.

Hurtado, S., & Carter, D. F. (1997). Effects of college transition and perceptions of the campus racial climate on Latinx college students' sense of belonging. *Sociology of Education, 70*(4), 324–345.

Hurtado, S., Milem, J., Clayton-Pedersen, A., & Allen, W. (1999). *Enacting diverse learning environments: Improving the climate for racial/ethnic diversity in higher education* (ASHE-ERIC Higher Education Report, Vol. 26, No. 8). Washington, DC: ERIC Clearinghouse on Higher Education.

Hurtado, S., & Ponjuan, L. (2005). Latinx educational outcomes and the campus climate. *Journal of Hispanic Higher Education, 4*(3), 235–251.

Johnson, T. (2017). DACA termination affects thousands on a daily basis. *Immigration Impact.* Retrieved from http://immigrationimpact.com/2017/11/14/daca-termination-affects-thousands-on-daily/

Kishi, K. (2017). Assaults against Muslims in the U.S. surpass 2001 level. *Factank.* Retrieved from http://www.pewresearch.org/fact-tank/2017/11/15/assaults-against-muslims-in-u-s-surpass-2001-level/

Kyriakides, C., & Torres, R. D. (2015). "Other than Mexicans," "Islamic Fascists" and the transatlantic regulation of risky subjects. *Ethnicities, 15*(2), 282–301.

Lawton, K. (2014). Latinx converts to Islam. *PBS.* Retrieved from http://www.pbs.org/wnet/religionandethics/2015/06/05/july-25-2014-Latinx-muslims/23669/

Martínez-Vázquez, H. A. (2010). *Latina/o y musulmán: The construction of Latina/o identity among Latina/o Muslims in the United States.* Eugene, OR: Wipf and Stock.

Martínez-Vázquez, H. A. (2012). The act of remembering: The reconstruction of US Latina/o identities by US Latina/o Muslims. In A. M. Isasi-Díaz & E. Mendieta (Eds.), *Decolonizing epistemologies,* (pp. 127–150). New York, NY: Fordham University Press .

Minikel-Lacocque, J. (2013). Racism, college, and the power of words: Racial microaggressions reconsidered. *American Educational Research Journal, 50*(3), 432–465.

Mitú. (2016, November 15). Revolutionary mujer-mitu [Video file]. Retrieved from https://www.youtube.com/watch?v=UD3xrHoRRz0

Murray, R. (2017). How many people are at risk of losing their temporary protected status? *Immigration Impact.* Retrieved from http://immigrationimpact.com/2017/07/26/losing-temporary-protected-status/

Nadal, K. L., Wong, Y., Griffin, K. E., Davidoff, K., & Sriken, J. (2014). The adverse impact of racial microaggressions on college students' self-esteem. *Journal of College Student Development, 55*(5), 461–474.

Nasir, N., & Al-Amin, J. (2006). Creating identity-safe spaces on college campuses for Muslim students. *Change: The Magazine of Higher Learning, 38*(2), 22–27.

Noticias Telemundo. (2016, November 8). Los musulmanes con más miedo desde eleccion de Trump | Noticiero | Noticias telemundo [Video file]. Retrieved from https://www.telemundo.com/noticias/2016/11/18/los-musulmanes-con-mas-miedo-desde-eleccion-de-trump

Pew Research Center. (2011). *Muslim Americans: No signs of growth in alienation or support for extremism.* Retrieved from http://www.people-press.org/2011/08/30/muslim-americans-no-signs-of-growth-in-alienation-or-support-for-extremism/

Pew Research Center. (2014). *The shifting religious identity of Latinxs in the United States.* Retrieved from http://www.pewforum.org/2014/05/07/the-shifting-religious-identity-of-Latinxs-in-the-united-states/

Reichard, R. (2015). What it's like to be a Muslim Latina on Easter. *Latina.* Retrieved from http://www.latina.com/lifestyle/our-issues/being-muslim-latina-easter

Rivera, C. (2014). The brown threat: Post-9/11 conflations of Latina/os and Middle Eastern Muslims in the US American imagination. *Latinx Studies, 12*(1), 44–64.

Rudolph, F. (1962). *The American college and university: A history.* Athens, GA: University of Georgia Press.

Sacchetti, M. (2017). ICE immigration arrests of noncriminals double under Trump. *Washington Post.* Retrieved from https://www.washingtonpost.com/local/immigration-arrests-of-noncriminals-double-under-trump/2017/04/16/9 8a2f1e2-2096-11e7-be2a-3a1fb24d4671_story.html?utm_term=.af09e2c73541

Santiago, S. (2014). 6 best telenovelas of all time: Marimar, el clon, and more. *Latin Post*. Retrieved from http://www.latinpost.com/articles/6284/20140123/latin-post-exclusive-6-telenovelas-cant-forget.htm

Schneider, A., & Ingram, H. (1993). Social construction of target populations: Implications for politics and policy. *American Political Science Review, 87*(2), 334–347.

Schuessler, R. (2016). Latinx Muslims at country's only Spanish-speaking mosque: "Islam changed my life." *Guardian*. Retrieved from https://www.theguardian.com/world/2016/may/09/Latinx-muslims-spanish-mosque-cinco-de-mayo

Stotzer, R., & Hossellman, E. (2012). Hate crimes on campus. *Journal of Interpersonal Violence, 27*(4), 644–661.

Tinto, V. (1993). Building community. *Liberal Education, 79*(4), 16–21.

Trump, D. (2015, December 29). Speech at Council Bluffs, Iowa, campaign rally [C-SPAN Video file]. Retrieved from https://www.c-span.org/video/?452469-1/president-trump-campaigns-republicans-iowa

U.S. Citizenship and Immigration Services. (n.d.a). *Consideration for Deferred Action for Childhood Arrivals (DACA)*. Retrieved from https://www.uscis.gov/archive/consideration-deferred-action-childhood-arrivals-daca#guidelines

U.S. Citizenship and Immigration Services. (n.d.b). *Temporary Protected Status*. Retrieved from https://www.uscis.gov/humanitarian/temporary-protected-status

U.S. Congress Report. (2005). Current and projected threats to the United States. Hearing before the select committee on intelligence. United States Senate. 109th Congress, 1st session, 15 February. Washington, DC: U.S. Government Printing Office.

USA PATRIOT Act: Preserving life and liberty: Uniting and strengthening America by providing appropriate tools required to intercept and obstruct terrorism, Pub. L. No. 107-56, 115 Stat. 272 (2001). https://www.justice.gov/archive/ll/highlights.htm

White House. (2017). *Executive order protecting the nation from foreign terrorist entry into the United States*. Retrieved from https://www.whitehouse.gov/presidential-actions/executive-order-protecting-nation-foreign-terrorist-entry-united-states/

Zainiddinov, H. (2016). Racial and ethnic differences in perceptions of discrimination among Muslim Americans. *Ethnic and Racial Studies, 39*(15), 2701–2721.

8

A HOME AWAY FROM HOME

Community Countering Challenges

Abiya Ahmed and Cassie Garcia

Higher education institutions have seen a surge in diversity initiatives in the past few decades, with intentional efforts being made to make universities and colleges more inclusive of various kinds of student populations. Accordingly, research on diversity in higher education has sought to understand both the effect of these initiatives and what more could be done to successfully promote diversity. Much of this research has focused on class, race/ethnicity, and gender as defining factors, as well as who benefits from this diversity (Warikoo, 2016). Some research has shown how racial and ethnic diversity primarily benefits White students, who see minorities as a "resource" from whom they can gain cultural and social capital (Cole, 2007; Warikoo, 2016). Other research has examined the role of socioeconomic status and racial diversity in forming friendships, identities, and social life in college (Antonio, 2001; Mullen, 2010; Stuber, 2011).

However, until recently (Astin et al., 2005), religious diversity has not received much attention, by either institutions or academics. Jacobsen and Jacobsen (2008) illustrate that religion and spirituality continue to be important aspects of students' lives, which universities cannot and should not ignore. Eboo Patel (2007) makes a similar argument, noting that religion is a significant identity marker for college students and can no longer be neglected in conversations about diversity. To this end, his organization, the Interfaith Youth Core (IFYC), intentionally promotes programs and research initiatives to include religion and faith in the broader diversity conversation, illustrating how it benefits not only students and institutions but also broader civic engagement goals (Patel & Meyer, 2011). IFYC has also supported nationwide surveys of college students that have shed light on how institutional legacies of inclusion, structural diversity, and campus climate influence students' ideas about religion and spirituality, as well as engagement with those who are religious and spiritual and those who are not (A.B. Rockenbach & Mayhew, 2013). Additionally, other researchers have offered models for student affairs personnel to be successfully trained in addressing issues of religion, secularism, pluralism, and interfaith cooperation (Kocet & Stewart, 2011; Stedman, 2011).

Religious and interfaith diversity in higher education, therefore, has now become a focus of both academic and institutional attention (Small & Bowman, 2012). Such attention has become more pronounced in the wake of the November 2016 elections and Donald Trump's presidency, which have caused heightened awareness and insecurity among religious minorities such as Jews and Muslims. For Muslims in particular, Trump's anti-Muslim rhetoric and the Muslim travel ban (Beirich, 2018; Johnson & Hauslohner, 2017) have had significant impact. In this context, one area that deserves more consideration is how Muslim students are faring on college campuses and what kinds of structural support institutions can offer to them, especially given such a divisive political climate.

In this chapter, we review some of the extant literature on Muslim college students in higher education, with special attention to identity development and experiences, gender issues, mental health, and external attitudes toward Muslims. We follow that with a case study of how one student affairs–run organization—the Markaz Resource Center at Stanford University—addresses some of the issues raised in the literature and serves as a "home away from home" by creating community for Stanford Muslim-identifying students (as well as for those who do not identify as Muslim). Finally, we conclude with some implications for policy and practice and discussion questions.

Muslim Students in Higher Education

Research on Muslim students in higher education is not entirely absent, but requires further inquiry. As Cole and Ahmadi (2010) argue, Muslim students have been involved extensively in interactional diversity on campus, even as they report lower levels of satisfaction with their educational experiences. We have some idea of what these experiences might be, based on the literature discussed in the following sections, but several questions remain unanswered, particularly in terms of what top-down initiatives institutions can take toward enhancing the college experience for Muslim students.

Identity Development and Life on Campus

One of the earliest studies done in a post-9/11 context was Peek's (2005) research on Muslim college students' identity development, in which she illustrates how second-generation American Muslims develop a Muslim identity through three stages: ascribed, chosen, and declared. In particular, she notes how an event like 9/11 can cause religion to play a more salient role in these students' identities, as they feel the need to assert their Muslim-ness, both for positive self-perception and for correcting misconceptions. Chaudhury and Miller (2008) also explored identity formation, specifically among Bangladeshi American Muslim adolescents. In relation to higher education, they note how, in seeking to further their Muslim identity, some of these students attempt to create "safe havens" on campus, where they feel more connected to their religious selves. In their study, one student actively creates a Muslim Student Association on his campus, while also getting the university to hire a chaplain to address their needs.

In addition, construction of a Muslim "other" also affects how Muslim students situate their own identities (A.I. Ali, 2014). In terms of navigating identities, social life, and discrimination, Shammas (2009) found that perceived discrimination leads to ethnic and religious clustering among Arab and Muslim community college students. Shammas (2017) also argues in a later analysis how some of these students might underreport discrimination, arguing for different methodologies such as focus groups, interviews, and similar qualitative approaches to better understand the experiences of this population. On this issue, Ahmadi (2011) has shown how the USA PATRIOT Act affected Muslim students in higher education, not only through increased government surveillance or restriction on visas but also in ways such as limitations on academic freedom and speech.

Muslim Women on Campus

In a pre-9/11 context, Cole and Ahmadi (2003) studied the experiences of Muslim women who veil on college campuses, exploring how peer interactions, misconceptions, and these women's own changing ideas about what makes a "good Muslim" led to some of them deciding to unveil. In contrast, Williams and Vashi (2007), who study the hijab, or the veil, among college-age American Muslim women, note how it functions for them as not only a religious symbol but also a social one, empowering them to be more independent and participate in public life both in and out of college. The role of the hijab in the lives of Muslim women college students, therefore, remains nuanced. As Seggie and Sanford (2010) illustrate in their case study of Muslim students at four Christian colleges, veiled Muslim students find their college environment welcoming but do experience mild exclusion and marginalization. Relatedly, Mir (2014) has conducted perhaps the most detailed study of Muslim women undergraduates, in which she examines how these students are burdened with responding to social pressures within a "hedonistic" campus culture. Her research offers insight into how these students perceive "normal" on campus, as they find it difficult to navigate through three unifiers of campus social life: alcohol, attire, and dating. Although Mir (2014) does not address overt Islamophobia per se, her research is nevertheless insightful in understanding how these students struggle to construct authentic identities, either compromising on religious principles or feeling denied social access.

Intersectionality and Mental Health

Another factor to consider when investigating the Muslim college student experience is the role of intersectional identities. Much of the literature focuses on the American and Muslim aspect of this intersectionality (Stubbs & Sallee, 2013) or on the gendered experiences of Muslim women students (Cole & Ahmadi, 2003; Mir, 2014; Seggie & Sanford, 2010; Williams et al., 2007), but there are other important factors with which Muslim identities intersect, such as race (Beydoun, 2016; Buggs, 2017), class (Beydoun, 2016), and distinct cultural mores like hip-hop (Khabeer, 2016), which also intersect across Islamophobic sentiment.

Finally, another aspect campuses and researchers should consider is Muslim students' mental health during college. Research on mental health in the American Muslim community in general is still in the nascent stages. There is, however, increased awareness of these issues in the last two decades, with special attention to stressors such as prejudice and discrimination (Haque, 2004). In their work on mental health stigma in the Muslim community, Ciftci, Jones, and Corrigan (2013) highlight the need for more research on this issue, with special consideration to factors such as intersectionality vis-à-vis race, gender, class, and post-9/11 discrimination.

Inevitably, Muslim college students also experience mental health problems that might be accentuated given these aforementioned factors. As Ahmed, Abu-Ras, and Arfken (2014) argue, Muslim students are not immune to risk behaviors such as drinking alcohol, using illicit drugs and tobacco, and gambling. They do note that higher religiosity curbs some of these behaviors and that group status and perceived discrimination serve as potential mediators of these behaviors. In their study on a sample of 120 American Muslim college students, Herzig, Roysircar, Kosyluk, and Corrigan (2013) also show that religiousness is positively correlated with religious coping and, in turn, active coping strategies with respect to stigma. In this regard, it would be useful to examine the correlation, if any, between Muslim students' sense of identity-safety and engagement in risk behaviors.

Attitudes Toward Muslims and Institutional Factors

How non-Muslim peers and faculty perceive Muslim students plays extensively into the Muslim college experience as well. Speck's (1997) research into professors' attitudes and practices toward Muslim students is an early example, illustrating how instructors' misrepresentation of Islamic practices, lack of respect for certain religions, and sometimes unwillingness to accommodate religious practices affected Muslim students. Some of his findings illustrate overt Islamophobia whereas others point to subtler forms of the same problem, such as the misrepresentation of Islam and Muslims in instructional material.

Nasir and Al-Amin (2006) also discuss Muslim students' sense of identity on campus in terms of how public Muslim practices (e.g., prayer, fasting, modest dressing, or not drinking alcohol) cause a sense of discomfort for these students. They, too, identify professors' knowledge of Islam, especially Islamic studies professors, as a factor contributing to how safe Muslim students feel on campus. They also note other institutional factors, such as a broader student community accepting Islam and Islamic practices, physical spaces for these practices (e.g., prayer or washing up before prayer), and access to *halal* foods (similar to kosher), as enhancing Muslim students' sense of safe identities on campus. Building on these recommendations, S. Ali and Bagheri (2009) offer several others, such as the inclusion of Islamic holidays on the academic calendar, the creation of spaces via student affairs where Muslim students can safely practice (e.g., a prayer room), the possibility of offering alcohol-free social events or experiences, and other more overt educational events such as panel discussions on controversial topics related to Islam and Muslims. They also offer specific suggestions for student affairs professionals for fostering better relationships between Muslim and non-Muslim students.

In this regard, A.N. Rockenbach and colleagues (2017) more recently examined non-Muslim students' attitudes toward Muslims, finding that non-Muslim students from minority groups (e.g., Buddhists or agnostics) have more appreciative attitudes toward Muslim students than those from majority worldview perspectives (e.g., Roman Catholics or Evangelical Christians). They also note that although institution type did not affect appreciative attitudes toward Muslim students, disciplinary majors did. Specifically, the arts, humanities, social sciences, education, and religion were correlated with more positive attitudes, whereas business and health care had the opposite effect. Additionally, they note that the presence of a multifaith center on campus had the potential to improve student attitudes toward Muslims.

As is evident from the literature, Muslim students on college campuses can face a number of personal, social, and structural challenges that deserve serious consideration at the institutional level. In this regard, we next present a case study of how a combination of student advocacy and institutional support led to the creation of a center that now serves not only the Stanford Muslim community but also those who do not identify as Muslim. Through this case study, we also present practical suggestions for student affairs and academic staff at higher education institutions.

The Markaz Resource Center: Creating a Home Away From Home

> *The Markaz being here at Stanford means that I have found a place far from home where I can actually avoid the feeling of estrangement I sometimes find in other places. It is also a gentle but very powerful reminder that there is a place on this campus dedicated to helping me achieve my goals and fulfill special needs that only the Markaz can provide.*

—Elham (pseudonym), Stanford student

In 2013, the Markaz Resource Center was opened at Stanford University to serve as a hub for students who broadly identify with, or are interested in, the Muslim world. The creation of this space was the result of over 10 years of student advocacy. The student leaders, members of the Islamic Society at Stanford University and the Muslim Student Awareness Network, sought to establish an office on campus that would support "a community that identifies with or has an interest, scholarly or otherwise, in Islamic culture, the Muslim world, global Muslim communities, non-Muslim minorities within the Muslim world" while also leading campus-wide efforts to make Stanford more inclusive for this population (Muslim Student Awareness Network, 2006, para. 9). Traditionally, support for Muslim students in higher education has existed within a religious or faith office, with ritual and practice as the key focus. Creating Markaz, an identity or community center for Muslim students, similar to those for Asian American and Pacific Islander (AAPI), Black, Latinx, and Native communities, was a newer innovation. However, as an organizational structure, such a center is uniquely positioned to serve the needs of this diverse and growing student population.

Five years after Markaz's opening, and with the addition of 2 full-time professional staff members and a team of 10 student staff, the space had grown tremendously. Markaz provides a space and a pathway for students to connect with their community, organize and lead programs for their peers, and directly impact the growth of their university through advocacy work. Markaz has developed a wide array of programs that seek to build community, encourage healthy identity development, promote self-care and wellness, and celebrate the rich heritage of the Muslim community at Stanford. Additionally, the center works with other administrative offices to address perceived anti-Muslim bias at Stanford and ensure that Muslim students feel a sense of belonging on campus. In this effort, Markaz has partnered with residential education to provide new interactive trainings for resident assistants on the needs of Muslim students in their living communities, advised counseling and psychological services in their search to hire mental health specialists who can provide cultural and faith-relevant support, and cocurated events during the month of Ramadan with the Office for Religious Life.

Advocating for a Community Space for Muslim Students

The experiences of student organizers behind Markaz illuminate several key strategies on how to advocate for such a community space. First, demonstrating an urgent and unique need for a physical space is critical, as university resources are often limited. It helps, therefore, to begin by identifying the target student population. Markaz attracts a wider range of students than a religious office might ordinarily. Individuals who frequent the center engage with and explore Islam in a variety of ways, including the devout, the questioning, the curious, the cultural, and the secular Muslim. Students of all gender identities and sexualities use, and work at, the center, and Markaz offers social programming for LGBTQIA+ students. Markaz has also created room for students who may not identify as Muslim, but have heritage or connection to Muslim-majority countries in our community. Once the target community has been identified, it is necessary to solicit their input on pressing issues or ways they experience disharmony or disconnect on campus. Examples from original student proposals for Markaz include a lack of adult mentorship, no access to faith-conscious counseling, and a dearth of relevant social and cultural programming. This feedback is important for the next step, which is to create a proposal for a community center that can address these needs.

Second, the proposal should also highlight the ways the community center will positively impact the entire university and connect these outcomes with broader institutional goals. A common critique of community centers is that these spaces "self-segregate" and stunt the growth of students. Although Markaz student organizers did not encounter this sentiment at Stanford, they did find that administrators responded positively to aspirational cross-campus goals. Students explained that, in addition to serving the needs of Muslim students, the center would work to cultivate an inclusive culture on campus; tackle faculty and staff diversity; and address other flash point issues, like student conflict around Palestine and Israel. Additionally, they believed that Markaz would contribute to the intellectual and cultural vitality of the campus by partnering with off-campus scholars, artists, and activists who identified with the space.

Third, it is crucial to be proactive in coalition building and providing space solutions. After the need for and benefit of the office were outlined, students organized a steering committee and began to look at space opportunities on campus. The Markaz steering committee included alumni and current faculty, as well as key administrators in academic and student affairs who supported the space's creation. Students then met with building managers to discuss possible locations. Through these conversations, students were able to learn more about ongoing space initiatives for development on campus and put forward suggestions to university leadership. With a broad coalition of staff and alumni supporting them and a tangible space proposal, the students were able to enter conversations with high-level administrators with confidence.

Designing Programs for Markaz Students

If creating a designated space at an institution is not currently an option, it still helps to organize social programs for students with similar goals of building community, engaging wellness, and shifting dialogue on campus. For example, Markaz's weekly social hour, Afternoon Chai, has provided an opportunity for students, faculty, and staff to come together, relate, and enjoy each other's company. Creating social spaces like this fosters organic community-building and mentorship opportunities that generate meaningful interactions. Reaching out to faculty and staff who identify with the community and offering them the opportunity to connect and meet with students is one way to initiate such programs. This low-energy, low-commitment programmatic effort can foster a sense of community and connection across university affiliations. It may also be an environment where students and staff can collaborate on future space proposals.

Similarly, Markaz's regularly occurring Chai Chat series provides opportunities for our campus community to come together, discuss an important topic, and learn in community. Markaz also regularly brings in Muslim art and artists to campus, as art education creates an easy entry point for all kinds of audiences to engage in learning. In the past, Markaz has offered film screenings, hosted theater performances, and organized gallery installations in the space to generate conversation and stimulate a more nuanced understanding of the communities that Markaz serves. In addition to broadening the perspectives of individuals on campus, this allows the center to support local nonprofit Muslim arts organizations and influential artists in the area while connecting it to the broader Bay Area Muslim community.

Working to Address Campus Climate

Community centers and student affairs officers supporting this student population should actively work to address Islamophobia and miseducation around Islam and Muslims on their campus. Although acts of overt racism and xenophobia do occur on some campuses, much more common are the dismissive, ignorant, or intrusive behaviors associated with microaggressions and tokenization. Due to pervasive media stereotypes, xenophobic political rhetoric, and rampant misinformation, students, staff, and faculty hold many unconscious and conscious biases around Muslims and Islam. As a result, students report encountering Islamophobic behavior in classrooms, residences, and shared public spaces.

Developing educational workshops and trainings for staff who work directly with student populations can help address these issues. In 2017–2019, Markaz applied for and received a grant to conduct anti-Islamophobia trainings for Muslim students and allies, as well as faculty and staff. These trainings include an overview of Islam and the diverse ways students identify with it, an explanation of Islamophobia and its impacts, how it manifests in the higher education context generally and for Stanford Muslims specifically, and strategies each target audience can leverage to address it. In this regard, providing specific case studies can better inform "how and what" is understood about the experiences of students and offer practical opportunities to build professional skills and generate student-focused solutions.

Conclusion

In this chapter, we have provided an overview of some of the issues that Muslim students face on college campuses and how programming and relationships at one campus community center help address those issues. The creation of Markaz provides a timely case study for how student affairs practitioners can work toward better supporting Muslim communities on their campuses. Student affairs practitioners interested in creating inclusive spaces and programs that honor Muslim students' identities can use this case study as a launching point for their efforts, which can then serve as a platform for long-term organizational change and the promotion of equity on campus.

Discussion Questions

1. How might a community center address the needs of Muslim students on your campus? And in what ways might this differ from the support provided by a faith-based office or a Muslim student association?
2. What are some external challenges you might encounter while advocating for a community space, specifically at your institution? Where might you find allies to help advocate for such a space?
3. What are some internal (intra-Muslim) challenges you might encounter while advocating or operating such a space? How might you address these challenges?
4. If a community center is a long-term goal, what might be some short-term goals one might put in place to support Muslim students?

References

Ahmadi, S. (2011). The erosion of civil rights: Exploring the effects of the Patriot Act on Muslims in American higher education. Rutgers Race & the Law Review, 12(1), 1–55. https://doi.org/10.1017/CBO9781107415324.004

Ahmed, S., Abu-Ras, W., & Arfken, C. L. (2014). Prevalence of risk behaviors among U.S. Muslim college students. *Journal of Muslim Mental Health*, 8(1), 5–19. https://doi.org/10.3998/jmmh.10381607.0008.101

Ali, A. I. (2014). A threat enfleshed: Muslim college students situate their identities amidst portrayals of Muslim violence and terror. *International Journal of Qualitative Studies in Education*, 27(10), 1243–1261. https://doi.org/10.1080/0951839 8.2013.820860

Ali, S., & Bagheri, E. (2009). Peer educators in learning assistance programs: Best practices for new programs. *New Directions for Student Services, 133*(133), 41–53. https://doi.org/10.1002/ss

Antonio, A. L. (2001). Diversity and the influence of friendship groups in college. *The Review of Higher Education, 25*(1), 63–89.

Astin, A. W., Astin, H. S., Lindholm, J. A., Bryant, A. N., Szelényi, K., & Calderone, S. (2005). *The spiritual life of college students: A national study of college students' search for meaning and purpose.* Los Angeles, CA: Higher Education Research Institute, UCLA.

Beirich, H. (2018, April 24). Trump's anti-Muslim words and policies have consequences. *Southern Poverty Law Center.* Retrieved from https://www.splcenter.org/news/2018/04/24/trumps-anti-muslim-words-and-policies-have-consequences

Beydoun, K. A. (2016). Between indigence, Islamophobia, and erasure: Poor and Muslim in "War on Terror" America. *California Law Review, 104*(6), 1463–1502. https://doi.org/10.15779/Z38S56B

Buggs, S. G. (2017). Dating in the time of #BlackLivesMatter: Exploring mixed-race women's discourses of race and racism. *Sociology of Race and Ethnicity, 3*(4), 538–551. https://doi.org/10.1177/2332649217702658

Chaudhury, S. R., & Miller, L. (2008). Religious identity formation among Bang-ladeshi American Muslim adolescents. *Journal of Adolescent Research, 23*(4), 383–410. https://doi.org/10.1177/0743558407309277

Ciftci, A., Jones, N., & Corrigan, P. W. (2013). Mental health stigma in the Muslim community. *Journal of Muslim Mental Health, 7*(1), 17–32. http://hdl.handle.net/2027/spo.10381607.0007.102

Cole, D. (2007). Do interracial interactions matter? An examination of student-faculty contact and intellectual self-concept. *The Journal of Higher Education, 78*(3), 249–281.

Cole, D., & Ahmadi, S. (2003). Perspectives and experiences of Muslim women who veil on college campuses. *Journal of College Student Development, 44*(1), 47–66. https://doi.org/10.1353/csd.2003.0002

Cole, D., & Ahmadi, S. (2010). Reconsidering campus diversity: An examination of Muslim students' experiences. *The Journal of Higher Education, 81*(2), 121–139. https://doi.org/10.1080/00221546.2010.11779045

Haque, A. (2004). Religion and mental health: The case of American Muslims. *Journal of Religion and Health, 43*(1), 45–58. https://link-springer-com.stanford.idm.oclc.org/content/pdf/10.1023%2FB%3AJORH.0000009755.25256.71.pdf

Herzig, B. A., Roysircar, G., Kosyluk, K. A., & Corrigan, P. W. (2013). American Muslim college students: The impact of religiousness and stigma on active coping. *Journal of Muslim Mental Health, 7*(1), 33–42. http://hdl.handle.net/2027/spo.10381607.0007.103

Jacobsen, D. G., & Jacobsen, R. H. (2008). *The American university in a postsecular age.* New York, NY: Oxford University Press.

Johnson, J., & Hauslohner, A. (2017, May 20). "I think Islam hates us": A timeline of Trump's comments about Islam and Muslims. *Washington Post.* Retrieved from https://wapo.st/2qCmaNc?tid=ss_mail&utm_term=.ad437361d4c1

Khabeer, S. A. A. (2016). *Muslim cool: Race, religion, and hip hop in the United States.* New York, NY: New York University Press.

Kocet, M. M., & Stewart, D. L. (2011). The role of student affairs in promoting religious and secular pluralism and interfaith cooperation. *Journal of College and Character, 12*(1), 1–10. https://doi.org/10.2202/1940-1639.1762

Mir, S. (2014). *Muslim American women on campus: Undergraduate social life and identity.* Chapel Hill, NC: University of North Carolina Press.

Mullen, A. L. (2010). *Degrees of inequality: Culture, class, and gender in American higher education.* Baltimore, MD: Johns Hopkins University Press.

Muslim Student Awareness Network at Stanford University (2006, February 8). *Muslim Cultural Community Center proposal.* Retrieved from http://www.easybib.com/reference/guide/apa/website

Nasir, N. S., & Al-Amin, J. (2006). Creating identity-safe spaces on college campuses for Muslim students. *Change: The Magazine of Higher Learning, 38*(2), 22–27. https://doi.org/10.3200/CHNG.38.2.22-27

Patel, E. (2007). Religious diversity and cooperation on campus. *Journal of College and Character*, 9(2). https://doi.org/10.2202/1940-1639.1120

Patel, E., & Meyer, C. (2011). The civic relevance for interfaith cooperation for colleges and universities. *Journal of College and Character*, 12(1). https://doi .org/10.2202/1940-1639.1764

Peek, L. (2005). Becoming Muslim: The development of a religious identity. *Sociology of Religion, 66*(66), 215–242.

Rockenbach, A. B., & Mayhew, M. J. (2013). *Spirituality in college students' lives: Translating research into practice*. New York, NY: Routledge.

Rockenbach, A. N., Mayhew, M. J., Correia-Harker, B. P., Dahl, L., Morin, S., & Associates. (2017). *Navigating pluralism: How students approach religious difference and interfaith engagement in their first year of college*. Chicago, IL: Interfaith Youth Core.

Seggie, F. N., & Sanford, G. (2010). Perceptions of female Muslim students who veil: Campus religious climate. *Race Ethnicity and Education, 13*(1), 59–82. https://doi.org/10.1080/13613320903549701

Shammas, D. S. (2009). Post-9/11 Arab and Muslim American community college students: Ethno-religious enclaves and perceived discrimination. *Community College Journal of Research and Practice, 33*(3–4), 283–308.

Shammas, D. (2017). Underreporting discrimination among Arab American and Muslim American community college students: Using focus groups to unravel the ambiguities within the survey data. *Journal of Mixed Methods Research, 11*(1), 99–123. https://doi.org/10.1177/1558689815599467

Small, J. L., & Bowman, N. A. (2012). Religious affiliation and college student development: A literature review and synthesis. *Religion & Education, 39*(1), 64–75.

Speck, B. W. (1997). Respect for religious differences: The case of Muslim students. *New Directions for Teaching and Learning, 70*, 39–46.

Stedman, C. D. (2011). Youth voices: Why interfaith work must happen on college campuses. *Journal of College and Character, 12*(1), 1–7.

Stubbs, B. B., & Sallee, M. W. (2013). Muslim, too: Navigating multiple identities at an American university. *Equity and Excellence in Education, 46*(4), 451–467.

Stuber, J. M. (2011). *Inside the college gates: How class and culture matter in higher education*. Lanham, MD: Lexington Books.

Warikoo, N. K. (2016). *The diversity bargain: And other dilemmas of race, admissions, and meritocracy at elite universities*. Chicago, IL: University of Chicago Press.

Williams, R. H., & Vashi, G. (2007). "Hijab" and American Muslim women: Creating the space for autonomous selves. *Sociology of Religion, 68*(3), 269–287. https://www.jstor.org/stable/20453164

Editors

Shafiqa Ahmadi is an associate professor of clinical education at the Rossier School of Education. Ahmadi is cofounder and codirector of the Research Center for Education, Identity and Social Justice in the Rossier School of Education at the University of Southern California. She is an expert on diversity and legal protection of underrepresented students, including Muslims; bias and hate crimes; and sexual assault survivors. Ahmadi received her BA in near Eastern languages and cultures with a minor in religious studies. She earned her JD from Indiana University Maurer School of Law. She focused on employment law, corporate international law, Middle Eastern languages and cultures, and Islamic law (Shari 'a).

Darnell Cole is an associate professor of education with an emphasis in higher education and education psychology at the Rossier School of Education. Cole is cofounder and codirector of the Research Center for Education, Identity and Social Justice in the Rossier School of Education at the University of Southern California. His areas of research include race/ethnicity, diversity, college student experiences, and learning. He completed his BS in finance and BA in philosophy at the University of North Carolina at Charlotte and received both his MA. and PhD at Indiana University Bloomington.

Contributors

Abiya Ahmed is a doctoral candidate at the Graduate School of Education at Stanford University. She studies the intersection of religion and education and is affiliated with the education and Jewish studies concentration and with the Abbasi Program in Islamic Studies at Stanford. Ahmed is interested in using interdisciplinary approaches to understand how individuals and communities learn and interact with religion in formal and informal spaces, with special attention to Muslim and Jewish contexts. She is currently examining how first-year college students form friendship networks, focusing on how racial, ethnic, and religious identities affect and are affected by these networks, with special attention to the role of intersectionality in this process.

Parwana Anwar is a former prosecutor, criminal defense litigator, and legal consultant. Her years as a deputy district attorney for Riverside County provided the foundation for her focus on criminal law, with cases ranging from simple drug possession to murder. While she runs her own practice at the Law Offices of Parwana Anwar PLC, a major focus of her work is advocating for the rights of the indigent as a felony trial attorney at both the Office of Assigned Counsel in San Diego and the Conflicts Defense Panel in Riverside County. Anwar earned her BA in sociology with minors in both law and society and history from the University of California at San Diego, and her JD from the University of San Diego School of Law.

Alex Atashi is a higher education professional and student services advisor at the University of Southern California Rossier School of Education. She was the first staff member to work at the Research Center for Education, Identity and Social Justice, where she served for over two years as the senior project specialist. Atashi is also a doctoral student in the EdD in educational leadership program. She completed her MA in postsecondary administration and student affairs at the University of Southern California and her BA in communication at the University of California San Diego.

Zulaikha Aziz is a rule of law specialist at the Asia Foundation. Her work focuses on international human rights, legal empowerment, rule of law, women's legal rights and gender equality, as well as civil rights, immigrant and refugee rights, and constitutional law issues impacting targeted communities in the United States. Aziz has over 15 years of experience working with leading multilateral and bilateral agencies, foundations, universities, and civil society organizations to further the goals and aspirations of the most vulnerable. Aziz earned her BA in economics and international development studies from McGill University, her MSc in development studies from the London School of Economics and Political Science, and her JD from University of California, Berkeley, School of Law.

Cassi Garcia is a student affairs professional and scholar-activist whose work and research seek to address issues of equity and inclusion within higher education. Garcia currently serves as the assistant director of the Markaz Resource Center at Stanford University, a space dedicated to supporting Muslim and Middle Eastern, North African, and South Asian (MENASA) students on campus. In this work, Garcia brings contemporary Muslim leaders, like activist Linda Sarsour, to campus, as well as organizes Islamophobia training(s) for resident assistants and professional staff. Garcia aims to ensure that all Markaz students feel a sense of connection and belonging. She completed a BA in Middle Eastern history at San Francisco State University.

Liane Hypolite is a Rossier Dean's Fellow in the urban education policy PhD program at the University of Southern California's Rossier School of Education. Hypolite is a research assistant at the Pullias Center for Higher Education and the Center for Education, Identity and Social Justice. Hypolite's research interests include college supports that improve the persistence and graduation of first-generation, low-income, students of color. She completed her BA at Brandeis University, majoring in both psychology and sociology, and earned her MA in education policy and management at the Harvard Graduate School of Education.

Bo Lee is a graduate student at Columbia University's quantitative methods in the social sciences master's program. Most recently, she was a project specialist at the Research Center for Education, Identity and Social Justice in the University of Southern California, Rossier School of Education. Previously, she was a program and talent development assistant at United Talent Agency, working on diversity and inclusion initiatives in the entertainment and media industry. She has her BA in international relations from the University of Southern California.

Marwa Rifahie is a public defender at Los Angeles County Public Defender's office. Rifahie provides direct legal services to individuals who are victims of discrimination from both the government and private entities. Rifahie is experienced in a diverse array of practice areas within the civil rights context including employment, national security, law enforcement practices, and prisoner's rights. Rifahie earned her BA in political science with a minor in Middle East/South Asia studies from the University of California at Davis and her JD from the University of Southern California.

Mabel Sanchez is a Rossier Dean's Fellow in the urban education policy PhD program at the University of Southern California's Rossier School of Education. She graduated from the University of California, Los Angeles, with a BA in sociology and completed her MA in postsecondary administration and student affairs at the University of Southern California. She worked as a campus visits coordinator for the University of Southern California's Price School of Public Policy where she was responsible for supervising student workers and organizing campus visits for prospective students. Her research interests include students' educational gains, issues related to religion and diversity, and student's intersectional identities such as race, religion, and gender.

Sama Shah is a recent graduate of the University of Southern California. She majored in both business administration and English. Shah wrote for *The*

Daily Trojan and served as a member of the undergraduate student government's advocacy branch as a diversity affairs delegate. Shah was also a PERE/CSII's communications intern, as well as an intern for the Research Center for Education, Identity and Social Justice in the Rossier School of Education at the University of Southern California.

AAAS. *See* American Association for the
  Advancement of Science
AACRAO. *See* American Association
  of Collegiate Registrars and
  Admissions Officers
AAUP. *See* American Association of
  University Professors
Abdelhameed, Rania, 69
Abu-Ras, W., 140
academic conference attendance, 69–70
academic conference boycotts, 70
academic freedom, 24–25
ACLU. *See* American Civil Liberties
  Union
ACT. *See* American Congress for Truth
Act of 1807, 76
African American Muslims, 117.
  See also Black Muslim Americans
African slavery, 76, 102–3
Afro-Latina, 120
Ahmadi, S., 81, 95–96, 139
Ahmed, S., 122–23, 140
Alam, Faisal, 93
Alcoff, L., 124, 125
Ali, S., 141
Alianza Islamica, 118
Aljarih, Faraj, 65
Alliance on Higher Education and
  Immigration, 68
alt-right hate group, 2
American Association for the
  Advancement of Science (AAAS),
  69
American Association of Collegiate
  Registrars and Admissions Officers
  (AACRAO), 24, 69

American Association of University
  Professors (AAUP), 24–25
American Civil Liberties Union
  (ACLU), 37
American Congress for Truth (ACT), 2
"Americanism," 77
American Muslims, 123. *See also* Black
  Muslim Americans
American Sniper (film), 1–2
American Vanguard, 29
Al-Amin, J., 129, 141
application processes, 71
applications, international, 24, 68–69
Arfken, C. L., 140
Armony, L., 43
art education, 144–45
Asiatic Barred Zone Act (1917), 77
Australia, 68

bad Muslims, 89–90
Bagheri, E., 141
Beydoun, Khaled, 20–21, 103
BIE. *See* Black Identity Extremists
birthplace, 3
Bism Rabbik Foundation, 118
Black college students, 106–7
Black Identity Extremists (BIE), 104–5,
  109–10
Black Lives Matter, 101, 105
Black Muslim Americans, 6, 88
  academic leadership for, 109
  Christianity and, 100, 102, 107
  CVE and, 103–5, 109–10
  discussion questions about, 110–11
  FBI and, 104–5
  in higher education, 107–10

surveillance, 36–39, 45–47
Syria, 52, 54, 63–64

Tabatabainejad, Mostafa, 39–40
target student population, 143
taser use, 40
Telemundo, 123–24
Temporary Protected Status (TPS),
    126–27
temporary restraining order (TRO),
    13–14
Theoharis, Jeanne, 46
Thirteenth Amendment, 76
Tindongan, Cynthia White, 88
Tinto, V., 130
TPS. *See* Temporary Protected Status
travel bans. *See* Muslim bans
TRO. *See* temporary restraining order
Trump, Donald J., 9–10, 79–80
    against "bad *hombres*," 126
    higher education and, 83–84
    Mexican Muslim women and, 124
    refugees and, 53–54, 55–56, 59, 64
    in 2016 presidential election, 124.
        See also Muslim bans; *specific cases*
Trump v. Hawaii (2018), 21–22, 56
Trump v. IRAP (2017), 16–18
2016 presidential election, 9
    FBI on, 80
    Trump in, 124

UC. *See* University of California
UCLA. *See* University of California,
    Los Angeles
UDHR. *See* Universal Declaration of
    Human Rights
Undercover surveillance, 1
UN High Commissioner for Refugees
    (UNHCR), 59–60, 62
United Nations Charter, 57
United States (U.S.)
    college founding in, 128
    Latinx/a/o Muslims in, 121–24. *See
    also specific topics*

United States Refugee Admissions
    Program, 13
Universal Declaration of Human Rights
    (UDHR), 57, 58–59
University of California (UC), 26
University of California, Berkeley, 31
University of California, Los Angeles
    (UCLA), 39–40
University of California, San Diego, 30
University of California Campus
    Climate, 26
University of Chicago, 27
University of Hawaii, 15, 17–18, 109
USA PATRIOT Act, 128

Vashi, G., 139
Venezuela, 54, 55
Visa Waiver Program (VWP), 12
The Voice of Islam/La Voz de Islam, 118
VWP. *See* Visa Waiver Program

Washington state, 13–14
Washington State University, 65
Watched (documentary), 46
weekly social hour, 144
Welch, Jill, 19
Western colonialism, 89
whiteness, 75, 78
    PWI, 106, 107, 130
Williams, R. H., 139
women. *See* Muslim women
Wong, Les, 28
Wong, Y., 130

Yemen, 19, 63–64
Yusuf, Hamza, 100–101

Zainiddinov, H., 121, 122
Zaytuna College, 100–101
Zionist Organization of America
    (ZOA), 41
ZOA. *See* Zionist Organization of
    America
Zonouzi, Leila, 66

Also available from Stylus

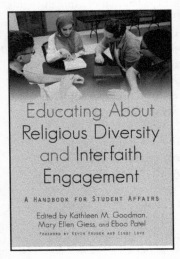

Educating About Religious Diversity and Interfaith Engagement

A Handbook for Student Affairs

Edited by Kathleen M. Goodman, Mary Ellen Giess, and Eboo Patel

Foreword by Cindi Love and Kevin Kruger

"If you dream about humanity bending toward justice, or relationships that nurture peace and even love, you understand that religious, secular, and spiritual diversity education is a critical frontier for higher education. History has taught us that college campuses are catalysts for movements of inclusion and human transformation—and Goodman, Giess, Patel, and colleagues implore us to design learning environments that champion interfaith engagement to this end. A treasure of pedagogically sound and practical wisdom awaits. I could not stop reading."— *Frank Shushok Jr.*, *Senior Associate Vice President for Student Affairs & Associate, Virginia Tech*

"The editors of this volume have produced a timely, thoughtful, and responsible effort that locates the importance of excellent interfaith practice within the good work of student affairs. Offering examples of effective cocurricular pedagogical tools—programs, activities, events, and case studies—designed to help students engage in productive exchange across worldview differences, the editors have provided an invaluable resource for institutional stakeholders interested specifically in inclusive interfaith engagement."— *Matthew J. Mayhew*, *The William Ray and Marie Adamson Flesher Professor of Educational Administration, The Ohio State University*

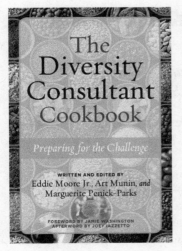

Diversity Consultant Cookbook

Preparing for the Challenge

Written and Edited by Eddie Moore Jr., Art Munin, and Marguerite W. Penick-Parks

Foreword by Jamie Washington

Afterword by Joey Iazzetto

"Most of us who lead diversity, equity, and inclusion work had to figure out the who, what, where, when, and why on our own. The Diversity Consultant Cookbook is a wonderful collection of voices from experienced consultants across the nation who share challenges they've faced along the way and great tips for becoming a successful consultant. This book is a great place to start for anyone curious about what it takes to lead others in this challenging work."— *Caprice D. Hollins*, *Cultures Connecting*

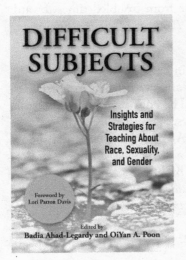

Difficult Subjects

Preparing for the Challenge

Insights and Strategies for Teaching About Race, Sexuality, and Gender

Edited by Badia Ahad-Legardy and OiYan A. Poon

Foreword by Lori Patton Davis

"Difficult Subjects could not have come at a better time. It offers keen insights and guidance without being prescriptive. It offers critical social analysis while still being pragmatic and accessible. As educators grapple with the tensions the current administration poses, this text serves as a beautiful and necessary counterbalance as we collectively try to regain our humanity."— *Nolan Cabrera*, *Associate Professor, Center for the Study of Higher Education, University of Arizona*

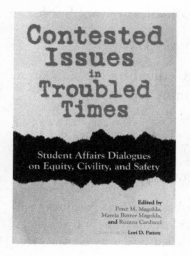

Contested Issues in Troubled Times

Student Affairs Dialogues on Equity, Civility, and Safety

Edited by Peter M. Magolda, Marcia B. Baxter Magolda, and Rozana Carducci

Foreword by Lori Patton Davis

"Contested Issues in Troubled Times invites readers to engage some of the most perplexing issues confronting college and university educators in the 21st century. As the contributors wrestle with provocative questions that defy simplistic solutions, they model productive dialogue and offer a rich constellation of perspectives for the reader to consider. This book urges those of us invested in the student affairs profession to think beyond traditional field assumptions and strategies as we construct novel and nuanced practices that will help us move from troubled times toward a promising future."— *Alyssa Rockenbach, Professor of Higher Education, North Carolina State University*

"In an era where overt oppression, righteous indignation, and name-calling are on the rise, an important skill for student affairs educators to practice is engaging about difficult issues productively. The contributors of this book model this kind of dialogue in thoughtful ways. Stemming from their previous innovative Contested Issues in Student Affairs, this companion book by Peter Magolda, Marcia Baxter Magolda, and Rozana Carducci adds a unique perspective on the important goal of building coalitions across differences."— *Stephen John Quaye; Past President, ACPA: College Student Educators International; Associate Professor, Miami University*

22883 Quicksilver Drive
Sterling, VA 20166-2019

Subscribe to our e-mail alerts: www.Styluspub.com